Producing Virtual Training, Meetings, and Webinars

Master the Technology to Engage Participants

Kassy LaBorie

PRESS

Alexandria, VA

ATD Press is an internationally renowned source of insightful and practical information on talent development, training, and professional development.

ATD Press
1640 King Street
Alexandria, VA 22314 USA

Ordering information: Books published by ATD Press can be purchased by visiting ATD's website at td.org/books or by calling 800.628.2783 or 703.683.8100.

Library of Congress Control Number: 2020946251

ISBN-10: 1-950496-25-2
ISBN-13: 978-1-950496-25-9
e-ISBN: 978-1-950496-26-6

ATD Press Editorial Staff
Director: Sarah Halgas
Manager: Melissa Jones
Content, Learning Technology: Alexandria Clapp
Developmental Editor: Jack Harlow
Production Editor: Hannah Sternberg
Text Design: Michelle Jose
Cover Design: Rose Richey

Printed by BR Printers, San Jose, CA

Contents

Foreword

I've known Kassy LaBorie for the better part of the last decade. Like many of the L&D professionals I see often at industry events, it's difficult to pinpoint the first time we met, but I do vividly recall one of our early interactions that built the strong respect and admiration I have for Kassy and her work.

When Kassy was at Dale Carnegie, there was a role being filled that I was interested in. It was a role tied to the organization's increased focus on using digital technologies, and Kassy and I spent a good amount of time talking about the company, the new focus, and—most important to the context here—her role in what was being built.

It was one of the first opportunities I had to really listen to Kassy talk about her work in detail. Unlike the well-rehearsed conference presentations I had seen in the past, this was just two L&D people talking shop. She described the work she was doing and what she was hoping to do in the future. Her passion was contagious, and our talks left me excited for the possibility of working together. I remember leaving one of our first discussions thinking, "This is someone who really gets it."

While that opportunity to work together didn't come to pass, I like to think I did get the chance to work with Kassy through her first book, *Interact and Engage! 50+ Activities for Virtual Training. Meetings, and Webinars,* co-authored with Tom Stone.

At the time the book was published, I was supporting the technology-based learning efforts of a local nonprofit. Much of the live training I supported used Webex, so Kassy and Tom's book was always on the shelf above my desk, ready to be referenced as I looked for interesting and engaging activities to include in the sessions I was building. It's a book that has plenty of highlights, earmarked pages, and Post-It flags sticking out of it as a testament to the practical solutions it provides me, and it still resides on my bookshelf today.

My personal journey as a learning and development professional took an unexpected turn almost a decade ago when I had the opportunity to join the eLearning Guild, known today as The Learning Guild. My work at the guild includes supporting our webinars and online conferences, and it has definitely made me look at a side of virtual sessions that I—like many in L&D—had not prioritized enough in my work: production.

For many of us, "producing" a virtual session simply means that we press "start" and hope it works out. I've lost count of how many sessions I've conducted, from design to technology-supported delivery, all on my own. While I was "producing" these sessions, in hindsight that production wasn't strategic or intentional; it was producing as defined simply by the technical requirements of making the virtual session happen.

It wasn't until I joined the guild, and began working with expert virtual session professionals, that I truly discovered what virtual session production means. One of the first things I noticed wasn't the feedback I got on our speakers; it was the feedback I got from our speakers, talking about how much the process used by our team made things run smoothly, allowing them to focus less on the technical administration and more on the learning experience.

There is so much that our virtual session producers and hosts do that had never been on my radar before, from the way they prepare speakers and attendees, to designing room layouts, to troubleshooting. It's all part of a strategic and intentional approach that raises the bar for virtual session production, increasing trainers' ability to deliver learning and performance outcomes in the process.

Had it not been for my work at the guild, I'm not sure if I would ever have understood just how important virtual session production is, and why it is its own critical skill set above and beyond what's required to facilitate a virtual session. But there's never been a resource that narrowly focused on the ins and outs of the production side of virtual sessions, emphasizing its importance in the work that we do as learning professionals.

Until now.

Producing Virtual Training, Meetings, and Webinars is the definitive guide for building a virtual session production strategy. It explores what makes a producer's role different than that of a presenter, the skills required to deliver upon that value, and the specific tasks that get delivered each step of the way. This book is a must-read not just for those who are interested in exploring a career as a virtual session producer, but for anyone whose work involves supporting virtual events.

I want to personally thank Kassy for placing a spotlight on an important role that doesn't get enough attention in our industry. It's my hope that by reading this book, and sharing it with our peers, we can greatly improve the virtual sessions we produce as an industry.

David Kelly
Executive Vice President and Executive Director
The Learning Guild
December 2020

Introduction

Virtual trainers, online meeting hosts, and webinar presenters, we have a problem: Engagement.

Web conferencing software allows people to deliver and participate in meetings, training, and other types of online sessions using their computer and an internet connection. This software is easy to come by in today's world, and meeting online is now a regular part of everyday work life for most people. This was already becoming increasingly true through early 2020, but during the COVID-19 pandemic such platforms exploded in popularity to support the significant increase in remote workers and virtual teams.

Even with such increased use, engaging virtual classroom learners, meeting participants, and webinar attendees is often a challenge. The list of reasons why is long, likely beginning with the presenter and the content, but almost always including problems with web conferencing software itself. In addition to planning, designing, and delivering engaging experiences, virtual presenters have to master the management of the technical side of this experience. This is generally referred to as the production of the virtual event or session.

The lack of understanding of how to engage online and the lack of skill in how to use the software effectively run rampant in live online sessions, with the technology distracting from the point of the presentation. The relevant story you tell to draw in participants is paused when you urgently need to troubleshoot a distracting echo over an audio connection. Gone is the plan to show your smiling face to welcome attendees if the webcam refuses to connect.

Let's Bring Engagement Back

Commanding the technical aspects of virtual session delivery is critical to fixing low online participant engagement. The art of virtual production combines a unique skill set that balances deep platform knowledge with multitasking agility, while at the same time calming everyone down before the panic can be heard through the muted audio connections.

How stressful can it get? I've seen people new to presenting online begin to open a session and forget their own names because they are so overwhelmed by the screen, the tools, and the lack of nonverbal communication from their participants. The technical tasks, referred to in this book as production tasks, can keep trainers and presenters from being their best and most engaging selves because they are not comfortable in the environment.

Producing Virtual Training, Meetings, and Webinars is for those who want to take charge of the technical aspects of running events using web conferencing software. Whether you are managing these tasks while you deliver a presentation, or you are the designated person to manage these tasks separately, you need to understand what it takes and all that is involved with successfully producing a live online session.

One of first things trainers and presenters learn to do is to "work a room" when conveying their messages to an audience in person. Tasks like connecting with participants ahead of time to learn more about them, or physically moving in a space to maximize the visual engagement and energy, are important ways presenters establish rapport, trust, and credibility. Connecting with live online participants and "working the virtual room" is something presenters and trainers must also do, with the added complexity of needing to first learn the features of the web conferencing software. Many presenters and trainers do not realize this at first and have not taken the time to develop the knowledge and skills to effectively manage all the technical aspects required to run an online session effectively. Engagement suffers as a result.

Recall the last virtual instructor-led training session you attended, the one where it started late due to audio problems. How disappointing was that experience? Remember the recent breakout activity you tried to complete, where everyone was too confused by the technology to get to the assignment and as a result just gave up. Or how about that time the entire session was canceled because the slides wouldn't load, and no one could figure out what to do. All these situations require serious attention because they are wasting the time, money, and resources of the organization and everyone involved.

In a survey I conducted of my social network, I asked, "What annoys you most when attending a webinar?" Not surprisingly, "presenters who are not engaging" was the most common response, closely followed by "audio issues" like echoes, feedback, and background noise. Additionally, a "lack of knowledge or skill using the features of the platform" was also clearly annoying. Misuse of other features arose too, like not knowing how to advance slides, use and pay attention to chat, or launch polls and share the results.

During the past 20 years coaching presenters and trainers to deliver online, I have found that the technology is often getting in their way. They struggle to be engaging because the technology stifles their ability to convey meaning and connect with audiences. I truly believe the inability to engage has more to do with the technical setup and execution than it does the mastery of the subject matter. Presenters simply do not have a chance to think through the content because technology issues take center stage.

We have, right in front of us, a huge opportunity to transform live virtual experiences by removing the barriers to engagement caused by a lack of technical awareness and expertise.

Separate the Content From the Technology

Virtual trainers, online meeting hosts, and webinar presenters, I offer you a solution: Deal with the problem head-on by separating the content from the technology. Instead of assuming one person can and should do everything, clarify what exactly needs to be done and then decide who is the best person to do each task. Consider in-person instructor-led training. Do we ask trainers to build the training rooms? Do we request presenters prepare lighting and sound, tables and chairs, drinks, and snacks in order to present their information to an audience? In most circumstances, we wouldn't even think of it. We have facilities teams to construct offices, and support personnel to manage the logistics and comforts of the entire experience.

This book addresses the key areas needed to put together a plan of action for technical success and online participant engagement. Through stories, templates, checklists, and examples you will find out what I have learned throughout my 20-plus years of experience producing and delivering thousands of virtual events including live online training sessions, meetings, and webinars. This includes what I have done for companies, organizations, and talent development teams around the world to address the inevitable technical problems that could have disrupted their virtual event strategies. In this book, I have curated a multitude of checklists, leading practices for success, and user-friendly step-by-step guides for immediate use and practical application.

The Terminology Used in This Book

For some, the idea of virtual production might bring to mind lights, cameras, props, makeup, sound, and staging, and let's not forget scripts, directors, and actors as well! While there is a place for all of this in certain settings, like large virtual conferences being broadcast around the world, high-profile speakers appearing live online in front of a virtual audience, or important company-wide announcements, these are not the types of virtual events and tasks I am referring to in this book. This book addresses the production tasks necessary for engagement in live online training sessions, webinars, and virtual meetings delivered by learning professionals and businesspeople across the globe each and every day. Examples of production tasks can include sending invitations with a link for participants to join the session; providing technical support throughout; testing audio, hardware, and internet connections for speakers and participants; and helping to manage breakout or small group sessions.

I use the terms *events* and *sessions* to refer to live virtual instructor-led training sessions, online meetings, and webinars. In my first book, *Interact and Engage! 50+ Activities for Virtual Training, Meetings, and Webinars,* my co-author Tom Stone and I defined the three types of events as follows:

- **Virtual training:** a training experience that most frequently has multiple participants and one or more facilitators (such as a trainer and a producer) together at the same time in an online classroom that allows them to communicate, interact, and collaborate with one another; view presentations, videos, or other content; and engage in large and small group learning activities.
- **Online meetings or virtual meetings:** much more than conference calls, with multiple people on the same audio or video call discussing strategy, a project, or other joint concerns.
- **Webinar:** a live presentation that occurs over the web. It is different than a virtual meeting, because while there can (and should) be interaction with the audience, a webinar presentation is largely in

one direction: from one or more presenters to a potentially very large audience.

The Production Journey

To begin your journey, in chapter 1, we start with a definition of virtual event production, the difference between a presenter and a producer, and the tasks involved with managing a webinar, online meeting, or virtual training. Chapter 2 identifies the capabilities to develop as you focus on growing your production skills.

As you progress on your journey, the next section focuses on learning the features, delivering the live sessions, and fixing issues along the way. In chapter 3, I introduce the two web conferencing platforms archetypes for the first time. It is my belief that learning to manage the functions and features of web conferencing software begins with this basic difference in mind. The various roles one can be assigned to run an online event determines how each platform will function for you. Chapter 4 outlines the roles and features available in most of today's web conferencing platforms.

Chapter 5 is a step-by-step guide to producing a live online event, complete with detailed checklists for preparing four key areas: technical details, content, presenters, and attendees. Chapter 6 is dedicated to everything that could go wrong and what you can do about each issue.

The third section of the book focuses on the people and the overall live online experience you have the power to create. Chapter 7 is devoted to designing materials with production in mind. Chapter 8 covers the ways to thoroughly prepare participants for an effective live online experience. Chapter 9 is an outline of what it looks like to partner with a person in the role of producer, the different ways people can help with production tasks, and the importance of a rehearsal using the intended technology. And then in chapter 10 we wrap up the journey by identifying the many administrative features available that can help you expertly manage all aspects of your web conferencing software.

Producing Engagement

When I first began training online, I didn't have a producer or even a list of tasks that would have been designated as separate or different from what I was doing as a product trainer for Webex way back in 1999. It was my job to teach the suite of online meeting products to the new clients, and I was to do it on my own. The production tasks were simply part of the job, and they were also the topic of what we were teaching in the classes, so they didn't show up to me as a special set of tasks necessary in order to be effective. It wasn't until I began working with clients—to assist them as they delivered their own training topics in the same way they had seen me deliver my training on the Webex products—that the production tasks became more clearly defined.

For example, as soon as clients wanted to deliver customer service training via their new Webex Training Center platform, they needed to fully grasp what options were available to them. Common learning activities like how to conduct discussions, launch surveys, and allow small group work were not only part of the content design but also now needed a technical approach as well. Once they understood what options were available in their online training software, it was then necessary to focus on how each feature functioned; in other words, where, how, and when to click on them. Presenters, trainers, salespeople, and others were being asked to focus on technology details in addition to content and session outcome details. For many, it is overwhelming, so much so that they simply do not use the features of the web conferencing platform at all, opting instead for a simple sharing of slides with a call for questions at the end.

It is no wonder we have engagement issues with virtual training, meetings, and webinars, but it is my intention with this book to provide you with the knowledge and skills you need to expertly manage all the technical aspects of your platform with ease. It's through the stories of my mistakes and successes along the way, the checklists that keep me on track, and the examples of how to make it all come together that I will provide you with the support, guidance, and encouragement to become the most incredible producer of virtual training, meetings, and webinars the world has ever seen!

SECTION 1
Getting Started

What Is Virtual Training, Meeting, and Webinar Production?

In This Chapter

- ○ Virtual session production defined
- ○ The difference between a presenter and a producer
- ○ Session types and the most common production tasks for each

Have you ever led a virtual training session, webinar, or online meeting and found yourself happily delivering the content only to have a participant drop off and frantically message you about how to get back on? Or, you're in the middle of speaking when your audio cuts off and you need to troubleshoot your device while still trying to engage the participants in the chat? Or, you bravely launch the breakout sessions and most participants go into them but then some do not, and everyone is confused so you decide to forget the whole thing and lecture instead? The scenarios I've just described illustrate the convergence of virtual session facilitation and production.

By now, most trainers, presenters, and meeting leaders have facilitated a virtual session. They very likely took what they knew about facilitating in-person and adapted that to the online setting. But while much attention in books, articles, and webinars is paid to the facilitation side of virtual sessions, significantly less is devoted to producing them. I've written this book to rectify this gap. So, what is virtual training, meeting, and webinar production?

Virtual session production—the key to engagement for online trainers, presenters, and meeting leaders—is the planning, setup, in-session management, and follow-up of all the logistical and technical details required for a successful and engaging virtual event. Production refers to the tasks required to deliver an online training, webinar, or meeting that are not directly connected to the content, but rather to the delivery of it in the live online environment. A simple breakdown of who is doing what is presented in Figure 1-1.

Figure 1-1. Presenting Versus Producing Virtual Sessions

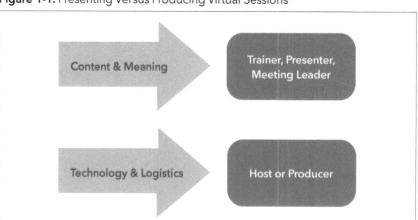

It is the responsibility of the trainer to take the lead on the learning content, the participant's connection to it, and ideally how they make meaning and apply it to their real-world environments. Likewise, it is the responsibility of the presenter to command presentation messaging and inspire audience members to action or other intended outcomes. And in the case of meetings, a meeting leader or facilitator takes the lead on agenda items and discussions related to the topics at hand.

But virtual classroom sessions, webinars, and meetings all require technical setup and focus that is not necessarily within the knowledge or skill set of the trainers, presenters, and meeting facilitators leading them. An individual who performs these tasks is often referred to as a producer. Other titles for those who perform production tasks include but are not limited to host, moderator, virtual classroom assistant, and event specialist. This book focuses on the production tasks that someone in the role of producer might do or that a facilitator might be responsible for covering themselves.

Production tasks include demonstrating, managing, and teaching effective use of the web conferencing platform's tools; guiding participants to connect and manage audio; using chat to communicate; annotating whiteboards and shared presentations; and participating in breakout activities. These tasks support presenters, trainers, facilitators, meeting leaders, and participants during the preparation, launch, and debrief of presentations and activities during a live session. A person in the role of producer may help with engagement in exercises and activities by role playing, commenting in chat, participating during discussions, and assisting with progress checks as needed.

Let's look at what can happen when a training facilitator doesn't feel comfortable with the production tasks. To put online participants into breakout rooms, the trainer needs to know where to click within the online training platform and how to manage the process of getting participants in and out of the breakout group. Without that skill or another person assisting with setup, they would need to stop instructing to do these tasks correctly. They also need to set up the activity so that participants can quickly master the technical process of entering, working in, and returning from the breakout group to debrief the learning and make connections. It's a process of moving from content to technology and back to content to successfully deliver a small group collaborative activity. This back-and-forth makes it obvious why many virtual trainers do not use breakout room functionality.

Unfortunately, participants are not engaged online when the trainer dominates the session—they want more collaborative and creative ways to learn. The trainer who avoids using breakout rooms is not deploying a proven strategy of engagement, small group learning, because the technology got in the way. By removing the obstacle of using the technology, producers clear the way for trainers to do what they do best, which is to facilitate learning moments with content and with one another in creative, relevant, and engaging ways.

This rings true for webinar presenters and meeting leaders as well. Webinar presenters typically perform to larger audiences, sometimes thousands of people at a time. How can a presenter focus on working up energy and enthusiasm to inspire engagement if they must simultaneously troubleshoot internet speeds, sound settings, and system connections experienced by audience members?

Meeting leaders face timing and planning challenges. It is not uncommon to have a day full of back-to-back meetings. Added to their list of responsibilities, they must also log in to the online meeting site with leader access, locate the scheduled meeting, and quickly find the start button. Online meeting technologies continue to make this process smoother by adding these controls to calendar entries, but the fact remains the meeting leader needs to start a meeting in order to take control, and that usually involves knowledge of where exactly to click to initiate everything, even when those buttons are on their calendar. The point is, it's usually more than just clicking on a link; it requires some level of technical knowledge on how to run an online meeting.

Trainers, webinar presenters, and meeting leaders all face production-related questions during their virtual sessions. How well they master the knowledge and skills of virtual session production (as covered in this chapter and the rest of the book) determines the success and engagement of their events.

Production Tasks for Different Session Types

Production tasks and responsibilities are similar in some ways but also can differ based on the session being delivered. Expectations from participants, from the organization, and from leaders of the sessions themselves change based on what is planned for the session, as well as the level of experience of those who will be speaking. Among the common features within a platform, the production tasks that will be required are listed in the next section. Someone needs to lead the effort of ensuring each of these features and tasks are addressed and are working properly throughout the session.

Commonalities

Here are common elements of all virtual sessions. First, virtual sessions need a link for participants to use when joining a session. This is typically referred to as scheduling the session and is done by an account holder, often referred to as a host. (Refer to chapter 4 on platform roles and features for more details on logins and host accounts.) This can be done either by logging in directly to the designated virtual event site or from an account holder's email program if they have chosen to integrate the software.

Second, virtual presenters need a way to share documents, slides, and their computer screens with their attendees; this is done in different ways depending on the technology. Third, it is common for sessions to have a way for leaders and participants to be seen via webcams, to communicate via a chat messaging process, and to get some form of instant feedback, usually via raised hands or buttons like green checks and red x's.

Fourth, all sessions must have an audio option, and this varies depending on the setup of the virtual meeting account. The options could be that the audio is integrated, separate, open, one-way, broadcast, a teleconference, computer audio, or voice over internet protocol (VoIP), to name a few!

Management of the production tasks is required to fulfill the purpose of the session being conducted, whether it's a training session, a large presentation, or an online meeting. Here is a list of common production tasks that must be addressed no matter the type of session:

- Generate an invitation with a link for participants to join the session.
- Select audio options.
- Provide technical support throughout, but primarily upon joining.
- Test audio hardware and internet connections for speakers and participants.
- Determine session options such as annotation tools, lobby settings, and welcome messages.

- Test how to share or show documents, slides, and computer screens.
- Connect and share webcams.
- Communicate using chat messaging.
- Determine when to use feedback options like raised hands, checks, and x's.
- Track registration and attendance.
- Start, pause, end, save, and share recordings.

Virtual Classroom Training

In my book with Tom Stone, *Interact and Engage! 50+ Activities for Virtual Training, Meetings, and Webinars* (2015), I define virtual classroom training:

> "At its essence, it is a training experience that most frequently has multiple participants and one or more facilitators (such as a trainer and a producer) together at the same time in an online classroom that allows them to communicate, interact, and collaborate with one another; view presentations, videos, or other content; and engage in large and small group learning activities."

The production tasks of a virtual training session include those common tasks in addition to all the support and logistics it will take to deliver the learning activities planned for the training:

- Communicate pre-session learning assignments.
- Upload or confirm asynchronous assignments and content.
- Create logins to learning management systems or other required technology.
- Send learning materials and logins to participants.
- Test all systems with participants.
- Build, load, and connect all polls and tests.
- Plan for breakout groups and materials.
- Plan follow-up and check-in communication methods.
- Track participation and assignment completion.
- Finalize course completion, including required certificates, accreditations, and units earned.

Webinars

A webinar (sometimes called a webcast) as I define in *Interact and Engage!* "is a live presentation that occurs over the web. It is different than a virtual meeting, because while there can (and should) be interaction with the audience, a webinar presentation is largely in one direction: from one or more presenters to a potentially very large audience." Webinars are commonly delivered as marketing and sales events because they are highly effective ways to generate brand awareness and host product releases. Announcements to the company such as quarterly financials or meetings where all employees are being called together are another example where the webinar format is quite effective. Learning organizations often deliver webinars to share information to as many people as possible; when skill building training sessions will be delivered in smaller workshops either in person or live online.

It's not my practice to deliver a webinar on my own, given how many people are usually in attendance and the amount of technical assistance that is often needed as people begin connecting to it. Production tasks for a webinar are usually quite involved at the start of the session, slowing down in the middle, and picking up again at the end. Most of the production tasks will be related to audio connections when participants are trying to connect to the audio broadcast, computer audio, or teleconference depending on the type of audio that has been selected. In addition to the common list shared by all virtual events, here are production tasks specific to webinars:

- Perform a technical check (systems, hardware, software, location, connectivity) for all presenters.
- Perform a content rehearsal and logistical walkthrough with all presenters.
- Send out attendee materials or make them available as needed.
- Assist presenters and attendees connecting to the session with technical issues.
- Record the session.
- Plan a question-and-answer process, ensuring members of the panel know how to see questions and respond properly.
- Manage all role transitions, changing presenters as needed.

- Build, load, connect, run, and save all polls.
- Plan a process for follow-up communications, including the recording and any transcript information needed.

Online Meetings

Meetings require production tasks, but depending on the size of the meeting, they are usually nowhere near what a webinar or virtual training requires. A typical team meeting is likely to be smaller than 20 participants, perhaps only five to 10 participants. The common tasks listed earlier are usually all that need to be done and may not require a dedicated person to manage or moderate. Meeting leaders can manage opening a meeting once it has been scheduled, starting the audio, loading an agenda, and sharing on webcam and audio as needed. Some meeting leaders may require assistance with taking notes and saving files, but it depends on the needs of the meeting, and again, the level of experience the meeting leader has running online sessions.

An all hands, or all company meeting, on the other hand, is more like a webinar, given the likelihood that there will be a large audience in attendance and high-stakes presenters speaking during the session. I follow the expectations and model the same practices for this type of meeting as I do with all webinars. As mentioned, the common tasks listed earlier are likely all that is necessary, but it is possible the following might be needed as well, depending on the meeting:

- Save whiteboards used during the meeting.
- Save chat conversations.
- Take, save, and distribute notes.

Now that I've shared the key production tasks for these virtual session types, let's return to the question of what falls under the role of facilitator versus the role of producer, and the corresponding production tasks.

Differences Between Facilitation and Production Roles

When it comes to the actual tasks that make up virtual session production, it stands to reason that the following questions need to be addressed: What needs to be done, who does it, and when should it be done? Assuming the "content and meaning" is the primary responsibility of the trainer, presenter, or meeting leader, and the "technology and logistics" is the main responsibility of the producer, host, or meeting moderator, I have outlined the specific examples and aligned them with one another indicating who leads on what, or who does what and when.

Before breaking down the specifics of what is being done when and by whom, it is important to note that not all online events have or even require a dedicated person to manage the technology. This is of course where the challenge of maintaining engagement and managing the technology at the same time comes into play. Some presenters choose to run sessions alone and are successful doing it. Those who manage it alone typically have two things going for them:

- **Less technology to manage.** They have less to do and less people to do it for, as in the case of leading an online team meeting. It is the rare team meeting that uses formal polling or requires breakout session management. Most meetings simply require connecting to the audio; sharing slides, screens, and other visuals; using chat; and maybe managing whiteboard tools at most. Audio, slides, chat, and whiteboards are not that much technology to manage alone, especially for one hour. These features are also the first features to learn when using online meeting technology such as Zoom, Webex, or Adobe Connect.
- **More platform experience.** They have more experience using the online meeting and training technologies and they know how to use most of the tools without having to first think about them. I have been working online for more than 20 years, leading virtual meetings, training sessions, and webinars at least once each week. I was a software trainer early in my career, so I am accustomed to clicking on features and making them work, even if I don't really know how to use them in detail. I am comfortable with the tools, even if they are new to me. I can usually figure out how to manage the technology, but even for me, when I have an audience that is larger than 20 people, I will not work without someone helping me manage the production tasks. I don't want to risk participant engagement dropping off because I'm distracted by anything technical.

Like with the production tasks covered earlier, I break this down into the three main virtual session types: virtual classroom training, webinars, and online meetings.

Virtual Classroom Training

When learning teams are implementing virtual classroom strategies, it typically becomes apparent they need a person dedicated to managing all the production tasks associated with successful virtual classroom engagement. When asked who does what exactly, or what needs to be done specifically, it is helpful to have a list of examples. Table 1-1 charts the common virtual trainer tasks to facilitate a learning event and their accompanying producer tasks or production requirements to manage the technology.

Table 1-1. Tasks for Virtual Classroom Training

Train: Facilitate Learning	Produce: Manage Technology
Welcome participants to the class; get to know them and why they are attending.	Welcome participants to the class and help them technically connect to the session through audio, chat, and so on.
Lead group discussions.	Direct participants to the raise hand and feedback icons and watch for comments that may come in the chat.
Coach participants during skill practices.	Assist participants with using annotation tools, webcams, or feedback icons.
Ask questions to help make content connections.	Remind participants to answer questions by using the tools properly, such as chat or feedback icons.
Listen to responses from participants and comment appropriately.	Ensure audio is clear and is working properly.
Clarify participant questions, ideas, and responses to help make connections.	Type what the trainer and participants say on the whiteboard or in the chat.
Deliver clear activity directions related to the purpose.	Give clear technical directions to complete the activity in the online classroom.
Take the lead in the class by creating an environment that is safe, inclusive, collaborative, interactive, and effective.	Follow the lead of the trainer by ensuring the technology being used supports the safe, inclusive, collaborative, interactive, effective, and fun classroom!

Webinars

Webinars are sessions delivered to larger audiences where knowledge and comprehension level objectives are the goal. Since production tasks for a webinar are usually quite involved, I previously mentioned that it is not my practice to deliver a webinar on my own. It is simply too much for one person to do on their own, and having a dedicated person for technical support issues, as well as content management logistics, is the most effective way to ensure an engaging webinar experience for all attendees. Listed in Table 1-2 are common tasks for webinar presenters to share and inspire participants and the accompanying host tasks that support an effective experience.

Table 1-2. Tasks for Webinars

Present: Share and Inspire	Host: Manage Technology
Greet attendees, make general connections, and establish likability and credibility.	Assist attendees with their technical connections so they can hear and participate.
Engage the audience with thoughtful imagery, key points, and demonstrations.	Ensure visuals (slides and screen shares) are working properly for everyone in the webinar.
Ask questions to inspire attendees to think and respond.	Enable questioning tools and teach presenters and attendees how to find and use them.
Acknowledge and react to comments and ideas received via chat and feedback.	Help presenters monitor responses: Read them out loud or help draw attention to them in a pre-determined way such as raising a hand or sending a private message.
Poll the audience, providing clear setup and debrief of the questions and responses.	Prepare and upload or connect the poll, launch it, share the results, and save them as needed.
Deliver presentations and demonstrations that are effective and accurate, according to the topic and the audience.	Follow the lead of the presenter by ensuring the technology being used to deliver the session works smoothly and effectively for everyone.

Online Meetings

An online meeting is the one place where a producer is perhaps not needed, unless the online meeting involves presenting to a large audience, as in an all-hands or all company meeting. In this case, follow the guidelines and recommendations of webinars instead. So, although a producer is likely not necessary for online meetings, it does not mean there are not production tasks required to effectively lead and run them. Most production tasks are connected to the efficient setup and connection processes needed to run the meeting. Others include using the platform features to record notes, see meeting attendees, and communicate with one another in a way that involves attendees rather than boring them. Some common mistakes meeting leaders will often make include, but are not limited to:

- Excluding the online meeting link in the invitation
- Not setting up or communicating the audio connection requirements
- Failing to test internet connections
- Lack of knowledge of platform features such as notes, webcams, and chat

Table 1-3 shares the common tasks for meeting leaders and the moderator tasks that help ensure meeting objectives are met.

Table 1-3. Tasks for Meetings

Lead: Dialogue and Thinking	Moderate: Manage Technology
Welcome attendees to the meeting.	Help attendees technically connect to the session, including internet connection and audio.
Introduce the meeting, review the agenda and timing.	Share webcams, and show a visual of the agenda.
Encourage questions and seek clarification.	Confirm raise hand, audio, and chat work properly for all attendees.
Listen to responses from attendees and comment appropriately.	Ensure audio is clear and use the whiteboard or note-taking features for reference.
Lead interactive discussions including report outs, project updates, and brainstorms.	Use chat, whiteboard, notes, webcams, and audio to keep track of discussion results.
List actions and next steps, and plan for a follow-up process.	Use chat, whiteboard, notes, and audio to capture actions, next steps, and plans.

Conclusion

Having a clear understanding of what virtual training, meeting, and webinar session production is and the similarities and differences between the types of sessions, it is now time to take a look at what it takes to perform these tasks. In the next chapter, let's examine the specific skill set required of producers or of those performing the production tasks and how they go about developing these capabilities to support a live online session with confidence.

Reflection Questions

▸ What live online session experiences would have been more engaging if a producer had assisted or if there had been more attention paid to the production side of things?

▸ What is the most common type of live online session you will be delivering?

▸ Which of the production tasks for your main type of session will you need to learn first?

Virtual Production Capabilities

In This Chapter

- ○ The necessary technical knowledge and skills to effectively produce live online sessions
- ○ The best ways to provide support to everyone participating in your live online session
- ○ The communication skills you will need to convey technical information to a live audience so that it is clearly understood

You notice a free training session that a web conferencing vendor offers for its products. The agenda is a list of features and how they work—it seems perfect for what's needed. Yet somehow after you complete the training, you are not much better off than before. Why did this occur? I used to teach these classes as part of my role when I worked for Webex long ago, and I quickly realized that I needed to change my approach. The problem with those sessions is not the content, it's the delivery. I needed to share examples and stories of people using the features. You might create instructions for the platform that illustrate its features correctly, but if context is missing, and the presentation strategies are lacking, the overall experience does not stick. Setting the context helps people relate, and an effective and engaging presentation of details helps people pay attention. The two together enable people to make meaning so they can recall the steps required to use the platform when they need to. Producing a virtual session requires deep knowledge of the platform features, but the ability to then effectively communicate how to use the features is just as necessary to everyone's overall success.

The skills required of help desk and customer support professionals provides valuable insight into the expectations of someone producing a virtual session. On the top of that list are communication skills, the ability to learn quickly, troubleshooting and problem-solving skills, the ability to work under pressure, and adaptability, to name a few that are especially applicable to virtual session production. The list includes both technical skills and people skills, for good reason. It may come as a surprise to some to learn that the production side of things is more than knowing the technology in and out. It is as much about communicating and relating to other people as it is about managing the features of an online meeting software platform, the internet, and some computer hardware.

I surveyed my social network of full-time, live online training producers with whom I have worked for years and asked them what skills were most important to effectively perform their jobs. They reported they the needed to be technical, improvisational, versatile, patient, agile, efficient, clever, present, astute, and empathetic. It's these answers combined with many years personally producing sessions that led to me create this competency model. It's technical throughout, but it also reflects the personal attributes needed to help one convey technical information, in ways that resonate, often without the benefit of nonverbal communication.

When preparing to deliver a virtual training, webinar, or online meeting, the administrative, technical, and logistical tasks involved require not only knowledge of what needs to be done, but also skills to perform effectively. And whether you plan to do it all yourself, ask a colleague to assist, or hire a person to be in the role, these are the necessary technical skills and personal attributes one must focus on to be successful: technical knowledge, technical and participant support, and communication.

Technical Knowledge

The technology is first in most people's minds when given the task of delivering a webinar or virtual classroom session. In fact, concern over getting the technology right is often so high on the list of priorities that it leads to a lack of proper preparation on content and meaningful connection to the audience.

I learned early on in my virtual presenting career to make a slide for any poll I intended to run. I was so excited to use polling that I focused on how to create it, attach it, launch it, and share results without preparing exactly where I would ask that question when the time came. I figured I would just remember. It wasn't until the webinar was done that I realized I never ran the poll! I had focused on the creation of the poll, but not where I was going to place it within the flow of my presentation, making me miss the technical details I had so carefully prepared. The technology was top of mind during the preparation, but I also needed to learn how to use it once I had an audience.

That's not to say knowledge of the platform and its features aren't important. It is vital to ensure a well-produced virtual session. But is it also important to pay attention to how the content will be presented while using the technology at the same time. Including a simple slide reminding me to run the poll became part of my production process. A cue such as this helps a standalone producer know when to assist a presenter and it also helps a solo presenter remember what to do in the absence of a producer.

When considering what's needed for technical knowledge, it is helpful to break it down into three specific and most commonly needed areas: learning the platform, using it, and fixing it.

Learn

Naturally, it's necessary to begin by thoroughly learning how to use the platform itself. Since this can be quite an overwhelming task, chapter 4 is devoted entirely to the various ways to learn about a platform's features and functions. Please refer there for specific insight into processes and practices, including tips for the current and most popular platforms used today. The three most important objectives for learning any online meeting platform are:

- **Know all the features of the platform,** including the administrative side that includes logins and site settings, to confirm the proper functioning of sessions. Obtaining a proper login, one that has full hosting access, and then opening a session, is the first step to learning all the features of the platform. Join with a second computer to view the participant's perspective and see how objects look when they move, are launched, or are used in any way. Click on every menu item and button. Connect audio; test the camera; share documents and screens; create polls, chats, and breakouts; and test all the other features available.

- **Comprehend the purpose and function of each feature and role,** to provide accurate support before, during, and after an online session. Knowing how features are intended to work is the best way to support them when a session is live with an audience. It is also necessary when providing support if there are issues. This is obvious with features like chat and polling, but it's just as important in understanding the difference between roles such as host, presenter, co-host, panelist, moderator, participant, and attendee.

- **Stay current with feature updates and product changes,** paying attention to details that might affect the function and experience. As an example, Adobe Connect posts updates at 8 p.m. Pacific Time on Fridays. It is not an uncommon experience to show up on Monday for a live event, log in, start the session, and have the icons look different than the last time an event was run. Successful production of an online session requires staying current with the changes, which are a normal part of working in our internet-based world. Expect the changes and work on being flexible when needed.

Use

It is necessary to learn the features of the online meeting platform, but the art of virtual session production begins with the ways in which you choose to use the features to create engaging experiences. The production skills to focus on for effectively using the features of a platform are to:

- **Use a variety of features and tools to effectively support a live session.** Variety leads to engagement as well as inclusion. Often when participants first connect to a session, they do not hear what is being sent via an audio connection. Sometimes this is because it is a teleconference and they have not yet dialed in, or perhaps their sound settings are not yet permitting the transmission of the audio via their computer. Using the chat to communicate is an excellent way to ensure introductory communications are being not only heard, but also seen. It's also a great idea to have a visual on the slides or the screenshare to display this information. Using various features in this way is an advantage to live online meetings, webinars, and training; you have the options available, so use them.

- **Assist session leaders and participants to use the features of the platform as needed.** Focusing on learning an online meeting platform creates a depth of knowledge not many people have taken the time to obtain, including many virtual presenters who lead the sessions and are ultimately responsible for audience engagement. Virtual session production can help session leaders be better at connecting with their audiences if they use the features of the platform to see what is happening around them. Often presenters will share slides, speak, and appear on webcam, but less often will they pay attention to the chat, ask for a whiteboard to collaborate upon, or place participants into small breakout groups to discuss a topic. This requires more platform knowledge, and producers excel when they encourage and then assist session leaders to do more with the interactive features available to engage the audience.

- **Provide timely and accurate technical assistance before, during, and after sessions.** Sending information out ahead of time, such as system requirements and audio expectations, will help participants connect more smoothly. Planning to be live in the session at least 30 minutes before the start time is a leading practice for providing the best support possible. Doing so helps to ensure an on-time start and prepares the producer for the types of assistance that may be needed during the session. Paying attention throughout, and quickly responding to the help people require, is one of the most important production tasks to focus on because it is, after all, the most commonly expected task of someone in this role. Noting what happened and paying attention to what is expected to be sent afterward, is also a standard production practice for after-session support.

Fix

The top reason for having an actual person in the role of producer, rather than just expecting a trainer or presenter to manage production tasks, becomes apparent when it comes time to fix a technical problem. Things go wrong, and when they do the ability to manage the following is the most effective way to not only maintain engagement, but to also lessen the stress that inevitably occurs during these times.

- **Respond to technical issues quickly, accurately, and patiently.** This may look like a rewrite of the third point under "use," but it is actually a reiteration as it is arguably the most important skill a producer must demonstrate. The "use" skill is part of the before, during, and after phases; we've already discussed the perspective of planning and preparing for what might happen. Now, the notion is repeated as an immediate response is required when in front of a live audience. Responding quickly is key, as there is usually only an hour or two available for the program. Accuracy is important so that the response works, and the session can continue as planned. Patience is often needed because participants are usually confused when under stress. Paying attention to these attributes while putting platform knowledge and skills into use is the best way to be successful when technical problems arise.
- **Create alternative solutions during sessions when features do not function as planned.** When presenting in person, the best laid plans no longer apply if the projector decides to stop working at

the last minute. So too online, where alternate plans, flexibility, a positive attitude, and confidence are your best defense when features fail. For example, sometimes breakout sessions do not launch, or the audio connections planned for them decide not to work. If a trainer has small groups planned, then changing it to a full-group activity may not be as effective. Using the chat to have partners conduct a conversation can be an effective alternate solution. Another solution would be to have the teams call each other on a separate teleconference line while referring to their participant manual for activity instructions.

- **Recognize when technical issues may be caused by the administrative side of the platform such as logins, site settings, and role privileges.** Sometimes it may seem that features are not working or are unavailable, even though they were fine in previous sessions. Other times, a presenter may try to share their screen for a demonstration and the option to share is nowhere to be found. Or what if the start meeting button cannot be located, or a person is left wondering where to locate an attendance report? Each of these examples are not problems with the features at all, but rather indicate a problem with a login, a role, or access to features based on privileges. Logging in to the site with hosting credentials is key to properly leading an online meeting, webinar, or virtual training. Clicking the meeting link does not always prompt a person to login as a host, especially if they are trying to access the meeting using a link generated for a participant. Sharing controls is not always available to those who are not officially in the role of presenter, or if the privilege has not been specifically granted. Knowing the features of the platform, including the roles and what is accessible to each, is an important part of strong production techniques.

Technical and Participant Support

At the center of producing a live online session is providing support for it: supporting those participating, supporting those leading, and even supporting the technology. The technology needs assistance to perform tasks and someone to investigate when things do not work as intended. The people leading and attending need support to understand the best ways to make everything work and this usually means how to properly connect to the session, to run it, to participate, and to manage it throughout, even when it is working as intended.

I have worked with many first-time online presenters and trainers who simply do not know how the web conferencing platforms can enhance their delivery. I will often hear a trainer ask a question and fail to get responses because they have not indicated how the participants should respond. I pay close attention when presenters and trainers are speaking and provide support by quickly adding in a statement like: "To respond to Sally's question, please raise your hand and then unmute. Sally, Luke has just raised his hand." Producing includes the ability to analyze a situation, based on knowledge of how the platform works, and be ready to help people with what they need to be successful.

Connecting, partnering, and analyzing are the three behaviors needed to support the leaders, participants, and technology involved in a live online session.

Connect

Clicking start meeting, join session, or enter meeting room is typically the moment when the most panic sets in for those running webinars and other online sessions. This "go live, no turning back now" moment requires a deep breath and a belief that one's knowledge and preparation will be enough. For attendees, it's usually at this moment that they realize they should have read the email with the requirements before the start time. These tasks are involved in this step of the process:

- **Assist everyone to download, set up, and join sessions effectively and following all platform and audio requirements.**
  Communication ahead of time is best when it comes to assisting everyone to connect to a webinar. (Examples are provided in chapter 10.) If production tasks are going to be performed primarily by the session leader, this is the moment where it is best to have another person help. Most problems occur at the time an attendee joins a session. Often, the online meeting software needs to be downloaded

then enabled to function on their computer by clicking a dialog box that gives the program permission run. Additionally, audio needs to be connected, and if it is teleconference, participants need phone numbers and codes. If computer audio will be used, participants usually need more support to help configure it to work properly. It is very helpful to have a person assist for the 15 minutes before a session and the first 15 minutes after it starts. The bulk of the production support will happen during this time.

- **Stay alert throughout the session, confirming all systems are working as planned.** Once everyone connects, it is not uncommon for a disconnection to occur. For a variety of reasons, usually the result of one's internet connection, attendees lose their access to the online session. Sometimes it is a complete disconnection where they are no longer in the session, and other times it is just a loss of audio for a moment. Sometimes this is due to the attendee's internet connection, but other times it might be that the presenter loses their connection. And other times, it might be a feature that is not working like a poll or a pointer. It's important for a producer to pay attention and be ready to send a note in chat, display a whiteboard as an alternative, or speak up on the audio to announce what everyone should do or expect next, if anything.

- **Recognize problems and create solutions to reconnect participants and equipment if necessary.** As previously mentioned, things often do not go according to plan. However, this does not mean that the entire session needs to be canceled. In fact, finding alternate solutions to keep going is expected, as no one is interested in wasting time due to a technical malfunction. For example, in many webinars there is the option to join audio either by phone or by computer. If someone cannot get the computer audio to work, assist them to dial in using their phone instead. Another example would be when a person cannot locate the annotation tools to add text to the whiteboard. Request that they add their answer in chat at that moment instead, and then help them with the annotation tools at a break or after the session.

Partner

If a separate person is in the role to perform production tasks, then some plans need to be outlined to effectively work together. Teaming up to present to an online audience is engaging, provides at least two voices to hear, and creates confidence that the technology and topic are being managed with care and attention. These tasks are involved in this area:

- **Rehearse with event leaders to plan for readiness, including deciding who does what, when, and how.** A rehearsal is key. It does not need to be word-for-word from the presenter, but rather a walkthrough of entrances and exits. It's important to answer who does exactly what and specifically when. A producer should not reveal poll results before a presenter is ready to speak to them or send out links to a website or an article if the presenter has not yet mentioned them.

- **Prepare polls, breakouts, chats, and any other features needed to run a smooth session.** Most online meeting platforms allow for polls to be prepared in advance. Some allow for slides, layouts, breakouts, and other activities to be planned ahead of time as well. Prepare as much as is possible before the session, and if the platform does not allow it, then create a folder that is easily accessed at the moment of need to minimize any delays during the upload or sharing process.

- **Advise on appropriate presentation guidelines, software demonstrations, and other activities using feature knowledge and experience.** Because a producer knows the features of the technology so well, and has produced many live sessions, they will likely know what works and what does not. It is helpful to advise virtual classroom trainers on how best to set up the instructions on a breakout activity since it might be confusing for a trainer who is new to the environment. Other examples include providing insight on how best to arrange a screen to demonstrate software, float panels, or look good on a webcam. Each of these details comes from experience in knowing how the platform works and having used it in front of a live audience. It's only natural to share these insights in an effort to make everything runs smoothly, thus leading to less failures or missteps along the way.

Analyze

Part of properly supporting an online session is knowing what might happen based on what is planned to happen. Planning in advance (for example, a written outline of who is sharing when), preempting problems before they occur (such as knowing that breakouts are complicated to explain), quickly responding to problems, and focusing on solutions ensures a session will be successful. There are so many things that can go wrong, but combining knowledge and experience, and paying close attention throughout the session, will set everyone up for the success they seek and expect.

- **Preempt possible issues to avoid missteps, using knowledge of platform functions, event processes, and audience engagement techniques.** Computer audio, webcams, videos, annotation tools, and breakouts all tend to have challenges. The errors are usually from the users, but they are sometimes due to platform malfunctions or internet connections. Test these in advance, in a rehearsal, using the exact same computer, connection, and equipment that is going to be used on the day of the session. Join with a second computer to note what attendees see and hear. Always start sessions at least 30 minutes early, and sometimes an hour in advance, to test each of these common trouble spots again.

- **Respond to problems quickly, without dwelling on them, following up as necessary.** Try not to call negative attention to the problems as they happen. Note them, deal with it, and move on. Do not bring it up again. Focus on the positive and keep things moving. Following up later will help you respond more quickly in the future, and possibly even avoid it all together. Like any learning process, we can appreciate the failures later as confidence and skill are gained over time.

- **Create alternative solutions when things are not working as planned, clearly communicating any changes to everyone affected.** It has been said that the best producers demonstrate "grace under pressure." This means they are calm, cool, and collected even when in the middle of a great storm of problems. Supporting a live online session in this manner requires all the skill developed from each of the previously mentioned areas: bringing together the knowledge of what could happen, a swift response when it does, and staying calm throughout all of it, is the hallmark of an effectively produced session.

Communication

Explaining how things work, telling someone what to do to make it work, or describing how to connect and set up everything for success is lost on people if the communication is not clear, understood, and pleasant. Technical knowledge is simply not enough. And supporting participants is often as emotional as it is technical. Producers will be most effective if they can convey a tone of kindness and confidence during the delivery of an online session. Presenters and trainers experience stress due to the pressure to perform for their audience, and attendees can be quite upset when things won't load properly or if they become embarrassed because they cannot figure something out.

When I was leading a team of full-time virtual trainers and producers, it quickly became evident that the technically skilled people we hired to perform the producer role were not necessarily also skilled at speaking in front of groups, and in fact they were often terrified by the mere thought of it. Our new producers knew how to fix technical problems, but they froze when introducing themselves on camera, thus hindering their ability to provide clear instructions. They also became nervous speaking the technical instructions out loud in front of large groups—they had more experience doing one-on-one technical support calls. We made it a standard part of the onboarding process to send all newly hired producers to public speaking training to help them gain the skills to be comfortable speaking in front of groups in ways that were clear, energetic, and engaging. We knew that without these skills, the producers wouldn't be able to communicate expertly with presenters and participants before, during, and after sessions.

Honing your listening skills in a variety of ways including using the tools of the platform, presenting complicated information in easy-to-understand ways, and appearing professional and in control are all key focus areas.

Listen

Listening is such an important part of producing that it deserves its own section. The most effective way to respond to technical issues is to have listened ahead of time to gain the clearest picture of a path forward. Listening using technology takes time and practice.

- **Listen carefully to cues for action from the facilitator as planned and rehearsed, and demonstrate flexibility as needed.** Event facilitators are not usually focused on the technology, because they should be focused on the topic and their audience's connection to it. As a result, planned cues may get missed, so paying attention and keeping an ear and an eye out while a session is live is necessary and helpful. With time, experienced facilitators will learn how to be clearer with their cues, but distractions reign supreme. Be the one to manage those distractions by always carefully paying attention.

- **Listen proactively for extended gaps in the facilitator's audio to jump in should they be disconnected for a few minutes.** Recall a time attending a webinar when the audio went silent. What happened in that moment? Did you disconnect immediately, or did you wait it out? A producer politely announcing over the audio that everything is under control is exactly what is needed in that moment. It's also important for a producer to note when the silence is intended, managed simply by referring to the prepared plan, but paying close attention to the reality of that plan.

- **Listen empathetically via audio and text to the technology issues each participant is facing to help alleviate their stress and find a quick solution.** In the survey referenced at the beginning of this chapter, empathy was one of those skills the full-time producers said were required to provide effective production support. The ability to understand and share the feelings of a participant struggling to make technology work helps move the support process along efficiently. If done correctly, a participant is likely to forget the troubles and recall the experience as entirely positive, even if it started out poorly. Sending a chat that begins with, "I know this is not how you wanted to start this webinar . . ." or "If only computers always worked exactly the way we wanted them to . . ." will likely bring a smile to someone's face and help them to quickly trust their problem will be resolved.

Present

Public speaking is an important aspect of any live online producer's role. Often, so much emphasis is placed upon the technical knowledge and expertise that presenting to a live audience is minimized or even overlooked. A person could know the inner workings of the platform and have expert level skills trouble-shooting solutions, but without the confidence to convey these messages to large groups of people, and often while on a webcam, they will lose credibility, sound ineffective, and perhaps lose interest in performing the job at all. Accurately conveying technical directions, responding quickly and directly, and providing clear feedback are the key areas to develop when presenting production information.

- **Convey technical directions clearly, patiently, and concisely, via both audio and chat, as needed.** Technical directions will be the bulk of the presentation needs for anyone performing production tasks. Learning to convey these directions as clearly as possible will help increase effectiveness. Participants are often confused by all the technology involved in the session, thus making a simple and direct approach the most efficient way to ensure success. Too many words and a lot of detail will make a person stop listening. Focusing on what is most important and the key actions a person must take will help the most.

- **Respond to questions quickly so that participants are not waiting for resolution to issues.** Participants will feel like they are waiting or being placed on hold within about one minute. It may seem like one minute is a short amount of time, but try sitting right now and not reading or doing anything for 60 seconds. It is important that a producer is paying attention to the problems people may be experiencing and responding quickly, even if that response is, "I will be right with you." It lets a person know they have been seen and feel important. This is vital, because without participants, there is no need to run any live sessions. Note that if hundreds or thousands will be participating in the live online session, it may mean more than one producer is needed to assist.

- **Provide clear feedback to the facilitator after each session** about technical issues that arose, how they were solved, and how to avoid them in the future. An advantage to a separate person assisting with the live delivery of a session is in offering feedback about how well a session went. Both presenter and attendee have what could be referred to as "biased" feedback given the positions they are in: The presenter is concerned about the performance, and attendees are concerned about getting what they came for. A person in the role of producer has neither of these concerns and has an in-depth view of what happened. They can provide valuable insight about what happened technically, as well as how the participants responded to the topic, in a way that is deeply helpful for adjusting delivery style moving forward.

Appearance

All the technical knowledge, skill, and experience necessary to support a live online session will be viewed with less respect if a person appears on webcam dressed unprofessionally, has a poor audio connection, or worst of all, demonstrates a negative attitude while assisting participants. How one shows up is as important as the knowledge and skills it takes to perform the tasks of the job. Appearing professional, sounding crisp and clear, and speaking with confidence and positivity wrap up the final set of demonstrated behaviors. The top producers from around the globe take this as seriously as staying current with technology trends.

- **Maintain a professional appearance and work environment, regardless of whether webcam use was planned.** Webcams have become increasingly common and expected in live online training, webinars, and meetings. It is important to be ready to be on camera, even when it is not indicated or expected. This includes not only one's appearance, but also the office or space from which the session is being broadcast. Don't let a distracting background or an unusual article of clothing be the one thing that disrupts the webinar. Being well prepared to be seen on camera creates confidence, and feeling confident means sounding confident.

- **Use appropriate audio and video equipment so that sound and images are crisp and clear.** Think of the last live online meeting you were in where the presenter was on camera with an awkward angle or had a window backlighting them, blocking out their face. Or recall a webinar where the presenter's volume was so low that no amount of volume adjustments would fix it. In each of these cases, even though the topic may have been necessary, relevant, and compelling, the sound or view of it being delivered ruined the experience. Most attendees will not tolerate a poor audio connection. It is unacceptable and unprofessional. Ensure the audio and video equipment being used is current, in excellent working order, and compatible with the platform and the environment.

- **Display confidence and positivity toward the technology, facilitator, and participants, even when issues arise.** Think "digital body language." The sound of the live online session determines how the participants feel. Are they excited or bored? Are they stressed or engaged? The trainer and producer set this tone, and the use of the technology carries it through. Participants want to trust the leaders of the webinar and that trust can be earned by being positive about the technology rather than complaining about how it isn't working or does not have a certain feature. This is especially important when the technology is having issues, as a positive attitude can often hide that anything has gone wrong.

"Never let them hear you sweat" is a strong mantra I live by. Participants follow the lead of those who are in charge, so remember this even when it would feel wonderful to scream at the screen! I know because I have done it. If you really must scream, then do not under any circumstances forget to mute yourself first, and then come back with a positive tone and message of how to proceed.

Conclusion

This chapter detailed the specific capabilities demonstrated by those focusing on the production tasks to run a live online session. It is so much more than knowledge of how the web conferencing platform works. Paying attention to how that knowledge is used to effectively run a live online session is what will make yours stand out. Following is a checklist of all the virtual production capabilities for your personal reference. This checklist can also be used as an assessment when observing another person produce a session.

In the next chapter, we'll examine exactly how to learn about everything available to you and identify the different types of web conferencing platforms that exist.

Reflection Questions

▸ **Technology:** What technical skills do you already have, and which ones will you need to focus on learning?

▸ **Support:** Recall an example of excellent support you saw demonstrated in a virtual classroom session. What exactly did the trainer and producer do to support one another or the participants?

▸ **Communication:** Did any of the topics in this section surprise you? Why or why not? .

Virtual Production Capabilities: A Checklist

Connecting to online sessions, supporting everyone throughout, and repairing issues if they occur comes up in a variety of ways in webinars, online meetings, and virtual classroom sessions. A person producing live online sessions should develop their skills in these areas:

Technology

Learn

❑ Know all the features of the platform, including the administrative side that includes logins and site settings, in order to confirm the proper functioning of sessions.

❑ Comprehend the purpose and function of each feature and role, in order to provide accurate support before, during, and after an online session.

❑ Stay up to date with feature updates and product changes, paying attention to details that might affect the function and experience.

Use

❑ Use a variety of features and tools to effectively support a live session.

❑ Assist session leaders and participants to use the features of the platform as needed.

❑ Provide timely and accurate technical assistance before, during, and after sessions.

Fix

- ❏ Respond to technical issues quickly, accurately, and patiently.
- ❏ Create alternative solutions during sessions when features to do not function as planned.
- ❏ Recognize when technical issues may be caused by the administrative side of the platform such as logins, site settings, role privileges, and so on.

Support

Connect

- ❏ Assist everyone to download, set up, and join sessions effectively and according to all platform and audio requirements.
- ❏ Stay alert throughout the session, confirming all systems are working as planned.
- ❏ Recognize problems and create solutions to reconnect participants and equipment if necessary.

Partner

- ❏ Rehearse with event leaders to plan for readiness, including deciding who does what, when, and how.
- ❏ Prepare polls, breakouts, chats, and any other features needed to run a smooth session.
- ❏ Advise appropriate presentation guidelines, software demonstrations, and other activities using feature knowledge and experience.

Analyze

- ❏ Preempt possible issues to avoid missteps, using knowledge of platform functions, event processes, and audience engagement techniques.
- ❏ Respond to problems quickly, without dwelling on them, following up as necessary to report.
- ❏ Create alternative solutions when things are not working as planned, clearly communicating any changes to everyone affected.

Communicate

Listen

- ❑ Listen carefully to cues for action from the facilitator as planned and rehearsed, and demonstrate flexibility as needed.
- ❑ Listen proactively for extended gaps in the facilitator's audio to jump in should they be disconnected for a few minutes.
- ❑ Listen empathetically via audio and text to the technology issues each participant is facing to help alleviate their stress and find a quick solution.

Present

- ❑ Convey technical directions clearly, patiently, and concisely, via audio and chat, as needed.
- ❑ Respond to questions quickly so that participants are not waiting for resolution to issues.
- ❑ Provide clear feedback to the facilitator after each session about technical issues that arose, how they were solved, and how to avoid them in the future.

Appearance

- ❑ Maintain a professional appearance and work environment, regardless of whether webcam use was planned.
- ❑ Use appropriate audio and video equipment so that sound and images are crisp and clear.
- ❑ Display confidence and positivity toward the technology, facilitator, and participants, even when issues arise.

Section 2

Learning, Doing, Fixing

Learning the Technology: Two Platform Archetypes

In This Chapter

- ○ Identification of two web conference platforms archetypes
- ○ Understanding the challenges with each type of platform
- ○ An easy-to-use, three-step process for learning any new technology

My first question when learning a new web conferencing platform is always, "Is it like Adobe Connect or is it like Zoom?" These two platforms are used to run live online sessions and have similar features, but they are quite different from one another in terms of how they present information to a live audience. I've been teaching people how to use online platforms for two decades, and I have found it simpler to begin by determining the type because it helps you to understand the basic way content is shared before diving into additional details. Attendees usually connect easily and quickly in Zoom, and they also tend to be open to appearing on webcam. Attendees connecting to an Adobe Connect session more often struggle to figure out exactly how to join and connect to the audio, but once connected they are often highly engaged by all the ways a presenter can be creative with the layout of the content and activities.

So, there are pros and cons to each type, and learning the features and technical functions of a web conferencing platform is the first step to successful virtual session production. Whether preparing for a meeting, a presentation, or a training, the way the platform works and the features available determine how the session can be delivered and the type of engagement you can provide to participants. How does the audio connection work? What is the best way to share presentation materials? Are there webcams and how are they displayed? It can be a long list of features to learn to get the most out of the platform, but with focus and patience, creating engaging experiences for the participants is easily within reach.

Mastering the technology comes from experience with the platforms. Pressing the "start meeting" or equivalent button and connecting with a live audience is an effective, although potentially stressful way to learn how things truly work. Practice in advance is also key. Clearly outlining a plan for interaction with an audience will help build confidence using the features. Comparing the interactions to in-person delivery techniques guides the usage of the online features and helps them make sense. For example, in-person it's common to ask participants to raise their hand if they can relate, so when presenting online, use the feedback icons to have them do the same thing.

It is helpful to have a process to follow when first learning all the features of any online meeting platform. There are many features to choose from and each one, though they may be similar in purpose (such as connecting people from remote locations using an internet connection to share information), they are often quite different in practice (for example, the specific features available and the exact ways information will be shared). But before delving into the three-step process for learning new platforms, let's first examine the types of virtual training, meeting, and webinar platforms that exist.

Two Archetypes

Having run thousands of webinars, online meetings, and virtual classroom training sessions over the past 20 years, my approach to learning a new platform begins by first identifying the type of platform I am dealing with. The first question upon receiving a login to a new platform is, "Do I share my materials in the moment, or can I upload them into the environment ahead of time?" The answer determines the planning, preparation, design, delivery, and support of all interactions and activities for the sessions.

I've categorized the platforms into two archetypes based on their primary presentation characteristics: Revealers and Builders. Revealers require sharing the screen or the presentation materials and activities after the start button has been pressed. In other words, the session must be opened before most actions can begin or be revealed. Builders, on the other hand, enable pre-loading of presentations and other materials or activities before pressing the start button. In other words, content can be uploaded or built in advance and will remain there each time the session is accessed.

All the platforms are multifaceted with special features that stand out, like Zoom's superb video conferencing capabilities and Adobe Connect's brilliant use of layouts. They also share commonalities like presenting PowerPoint files, sharing screens for software demonstrations, chat for text communications, and polling for surveying an audience. Identifying these two archetypes helps to understand how best to create and support engaging live online experiences.

Revealers

The environment of the Revealers is one in which most interactions and planned activities will be shared with a live audience once the session has started. Typically, some form of a screenshare (desktop or individual applications) is required to "reveal" the materials participants need to see during the session. Platforms like Zoom and GoToWebinar are examples. When the start button is pressed, the presenter can share their slides, launch polls, and begin communicating with participants as they join. This does not mean that the slides or polls are not prepared in advance; it simply means that content is not put into or available in the live online environment until the session has begun. Some common Revealers are Webex, Zoom, GoToWebinar (and the associated GoToMeeting and GoToTraining), Microsoft Teams, and Skype for Business.

Some platforms like Zoom and GoToWebinar allow polls to be created ahead of time and files to be attached to specific meetings, thus making them available for launch when the session starts, and sometimes before or after as well. Others, like Webex, allow for polling files (.atp file format) to be created in advance, but they need to be uploaded and launched once the session has started. Each platform is different in the specific way its features function, but Revealers have the key characteristic of primarily sharing content once the session has started, requiring the presenter to share or upload materials at the time the session is live.

When working with Revealers, I recommend creating a folder dedicated to each session filled with all the slides, polls, handouts, and other activities in one place for quick reference since the presenter will need to access them throughout the session. It's inefficient and unrealistic to expect to remember where all the files are stored if they are in different places, so organize them together so there is one less administrative detail to think about when with a live audience.

Challenges With Revealers

Revealer-type web conferencing platforms can be challenging to use due to the very nature of the design of sharing one's screen to show documents, lessons, presentations, software demonstrations, and such. Many presenters have accidentally shared too much, unintentionally revealing an email, sensitive document, or private instant message during a live webinar. For example, I once shared my resume on screen with my boss who had no idea I was looking for another opportunity! These types of mistakes are so common in fact that some programs have a feature where instant messaging automatically becomes unavailable when in a meeting! This is helpful for privacy but presents a problem if instant messaging is used to get immediate technical support from a team of producers. (Chapter 9 delves further into using instant messaging to maintain production support with other team members when presenting live online.)

Another challenge is that it is easy to lose track of the planned interactions if it includes more than sharing a presentation. It's easy to forget to share other content because the presenter's screen typically goes full screen by default, making other documents or content not readily visible. The other panels, like the list of participants, chat, and polling, might get rearranged, too. They usually minimize or collapse on a floating or docked toolbar where buttons for each panel can be found. Sometimes this toolbar is difficult to locate. For example, in GoToWebinar it is docked on the top right side of the screen and collapses and expands when moving a mouse over it. In Zoom, a toolbar indicating "Stop Share" appears at the top of the screen; to find the other panels, it's necessary to mouse over that area for the toolbar to appear. Once the panels are floating, they need to be placed on the screen where they are most useful for the presenter. Sometimes it is easiest for the presenter to use a second monitor for these panels, so they are still viewable but out of the way. It is challenging to learn the best way to manage all of this with confidence. It takes focus on how things work, experimentation with what is most comfortable, and practice with a live audience.

When I first began using Zoom, I only had one computer and one screen. I found it challenging to float all the panels and still manage my presentation at the same time. I also could not see enough of my presentation once the panels were expanded. All of that changed when I began using a second monitor. I now present from my main computer and float all the interactive panels to my second screen. This gives me enough space to see the slides, and enough room to use the interactive features while presenting and training. Whether you're a presenter handling both facilitation and production, or a standalone producer supporting a presenter, I recommend you use two monitors for virtual sessions.

Builders

A Builder environment is different from a Revealer in one major way: The session and all its content can be preloaded or built in advance. Since it can be prepared and accessed in advance, it also remains in the form it was left in long after a session has ended, enabling presenters to revisit the sessions and rooms to see not only the content but also the interactions (chats, whiteboard annotations, polls results, and so on) that occurred. Example Builders include Adobe Connect, Saba Classroom, Blackboard, and Jigsaw.

It's a leading practice to build sessions and entire programs as templates so the effort it takes to create all the interactions and upload all the content does not have to be repeated each time a program is scheduled to run or each time a new trainer will be delivering it. Most Builder platforms have default layouts or areas for sharing content that are included with a basic meeting or training. Adobe Connect, for example, begins with three layouts to provide ideas and inspiration on ways to arrange the screen and choose to share content with participants. It's important to note that building everything ahead of time is not required in these platforms. It is also possible to start a session, connect with participants, share slides and webcam feeds, and conduct meetings without uploading anything in advance. The key characteristic of the Builders is that a link to a session or room can be generated, content can be uploaded in advance, and repeated access can be granted, such that all the uploaded content remains.

Challenges With Builders

The biggest challenge with the Builders is time: It takes time to learn all the features of the program, to plan the organization and the visuals for all the interactions, and to upload everything. There are many features and options included with these types of platforms, and it can easily feel overwhelming with so many choices of how to create a session. It's not necessary to use all these features, but to learn enough to take full advantage of them will take time.

Consider that when I led the training delivery team for Dale Carnegie Digital, we hired a full-time producer to partner with the instructional design team to manage the transfer of training programs from design to delivery once they were completed. About 40 percent of his role was building the templates in our virtual classroom platform, uploading all the content, and making all materials available for the training delivery team and participants to access.

Additionally, once everything is uploaded and the session is prepared, or recreated from a template, it can seem like there is little freedom to make changes. Creativity might become blocked because everything is there, ready to be presented. It's a challenge to make it seem fresh when things are the same each time the session is accessed. Also, in the case of presenters delivering sessions they did not build themselves, they may not know how to make any changes, so they just proceed as planned.

A third challenge with Builders is ensuring the file types in use are compatible. It is the nature of a Builder platform to prepare all content in a session ahead of time, so the files used must be compatible to be added. For example, not all file types can be shared into the content viewer in Webex or a share pod in Adobe Connect. It's important to check which file types are recognized by the platform you are using and to communicate with the design and technical teams so the files they create for your classes and presentations can be properly shared and displayed.

Which Archetype Is Right for You?

Often during my consulting or speaking work, I'm asked what my favorite platform or archetype is. The truth is that I don't have one. My priority is that the platform is easy to use and technically sound. Engagement won't have a chance if people cannot connect or figure out how to use the features. I choose Revealers for their ease of use and how quickly things can be shared. I choose Builders for their ability to prepare and set trainers and presenters up for success without all the preplanning effort being placed upon them. Performance is key: platforms without technical failure first, and choice of interactive features second.

Table 3-1 summarizes the differences between the two platform archetypes. An example of a reflection activity for each follows.

Table 3-1. Revealers Versus Builders (Live Online Platform Archetypes)

	Revealer	Builder
Environment	Shared in the moment of "Go live"	Uploaded in advance of "Go live"
Example platforms	<ul><li>Zoom</li><li>Webex suite</li><li>GoTo suite</li><li>Microsoft Teams or Skype for Business</li></ul>	<ul><li>Adobe Connect</li><li>Saba Classroom</li><li>Blackboard</li><li>Jigsaw</li></ul>

Table 3-1. Revealers Versus Builders (Live Online Platform Archetypes) (cont.)

	Revealer	Builder
Characteristics of the interactions	• Share screen to applications and content • Float panel and panes to interact	• Prepare the environment in advance (layouts, pods, rooms) • Import and preload content
Challenges	• Screen sharing makes it easy to reveal more than intended • It can be easy to lose track of what is planned since it is not all preloaded • The floating panels can get lost, or become confusing or distracting	• The prebuilt screens can seem overwhelming and difficult to navigate • When everything is preloaded and planned, creativity and freedom can seem restricted • Sometimes activities and file types are not compatible and will not upload

Notice that the reflection activity in Figure 3-1 captures what was learned and the impact of each person's learning. In a Revealer type platform, a slide with a blank table is created, and the presenter then shares their screen to reveal it. The annotation tools are used with participants typing on the shared screen. A presenter or producer must then save a screenshot of the table if they want to refer to it later. Also of note: The participants and chat panels have been expanded in Figure 3-1 so the presenter can see any activity in those areas during this time.

Figure 3-1. A Reflections Activity Example in a Revealer Platform

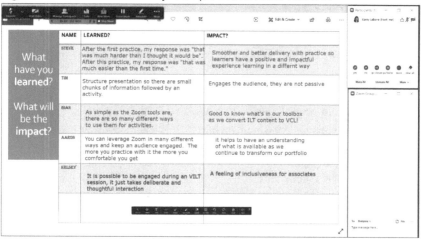

Figure 3-2 shows the same final reflections activity in a Builder type platform. The layout looks completely different, with pods for additional images that can be added to the layout. Further, rather than using a slide for attendees to annotate upon (which could have been done), I chose to use two separate chat pods for them to type their thoughts instead. The images can remind people of where they have been, and inspire them for future success. These images are not shown in the Revealer type example in Figure 3-1, though I did place them in the participant manual. Also of note is that by having two separate chat pods, the learning and impact are not lined up. As stated in the opening of this chapter, there are pros and cons to each type of platform, so design choices need to be made accordingly.

Figure 3-2. A Reflections Activity Example in a Builder Platform

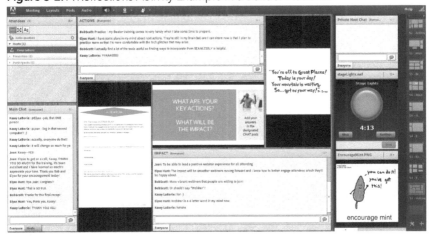

ACT: A Three-Step Learning Process

With the platform archetypes identified, the next step is to learn how they operate, and which features are available. Revealers and Builders alike have many features to choose from, so it is helpful to have a step-by-step guide for learning how to use them. Before we examine each feature in chapter 4, let's establish a three-step process as an overall guideline for learning any new technology. This process helps build confidences while also focusing on each of the components of a live online session: hosting, presenting, and participating. Use the acronym ACT to learn any web conferencing platform: access, click, and team up (Figure 3-3). In other words, log in and start a session, click on everything, and get some help to learn the participants' view!

Figure 3-3. Three-Step ACT Learning Process

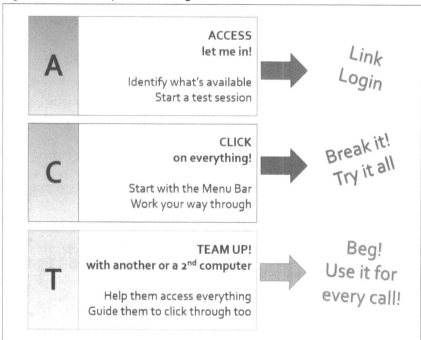

Access

Begin by identifying the process for logging in as a user who has some form of host status. Each platform has its own name for this role, but what is key is that this role can set up and schedule sessions; edit, cancel, and start them; invite participants; and access any behind-the-scenes features such as recordings and reports. Most live online platforms have a link from which the live online sessions run, and a login to the site that hosts it. And most online meeting platforms also have options to integrate this process with email programs and learning management systems. Note that some features may be limited if you're setting up and scheduling sessions from email programs. Learning management system integrations tend to have their own set of features. It's a leading practice to also have access to review the original web conferencing site in case there are additional options you'd like to use for your programming.

Logins can quickly become complicated, but what's important at this stage is understanding the logins available for the platform you are using. There are generally three types of logins: a host type to schedule and set up sessions, a presenter type to be a presenter in someone else's session, and sometimes a participant type to allow access to a site and the sessions attended. Presenter and participant logins do not usually have enough access to fully run a session because they are created to allow quick access to participate in someone else's session.

A common technical problem people face is not being able to locate the start button for their meeting. This means they are not logged in to the site with the proper access to host that session. Or, they don't have the proper credentials to start the session. (Refer to chapter 10 for a checklist of questions to answer regarding logins.)

Click

After determining the host account, it's now time to use that login and click on everything. Click on the profile and read through all the options. Click on every menu option available. Typical site options include settings for the user account like a profile picture and location information, and audio settings like a teleconference profile. There are usually places for scheduling meetings, establishing meeting settings, and accessing recordings and various reports. Sometimes there are special locations for the storage of files, creation of tests and polls, setup of virtual labs, and the general archiving of past sessions and their content.

After clicking through all the settings and options for the host login, schedule a meeting, training, event, or session, and start it. Some platforms have a quick button for this that allows an instant session to be opened. Regardless, create a session and start it to get in and click through all the in-meeting options available. Once the session is open, start the audio and connect to it, paying attention to the experience. Is there a teleconference option, a computer audio option, or both? How is a presentation shared? Where is the chat located? What are all the menu options, and do the panels or panes move, resize, collapse, or expand? What are the in-meeting settings or preferences, and where is the "end meeting" button? Click on every menu option and button inside the session. Some of the options will not be available until a participant joins, which is why the third part of the ACT process is team up.

Team Up

Team up has two parts: joining from a second computer as an attendee for your own personal view and partnering with colleagues or friends to practice. As mentioned, some features are not activated until a participant has joined the session. This is most often the case with polling and breakout sessions. The buttons may be there, but they are not active until another person has joined the session.

Additionally, it is common for the participant view of online meetings to look different from the host or presenter's view. Each platform is different, so it is imperative to log in with a second computer to see exactly what this looks like for your attendees. For example, when launching a poll, what does the participant see exactly? When does it show up and where? What do they click on? Does it go away or stay in their view until they minimize it? Where do the results display? It is highly recommended to continue to use this practice each time you run a live session as well. When participants have questions about the interface of the platform, remember that a host might have a different view, so in order to provide proper support, use the second attendee computer as a reference for answering these types of questions.

It is sometimes helpful to have not only a second computer logged in, but a different type of computer. If you use a Mac, then log in using a PC for your second one. It may also be useful to join as an attendee using a mobile device if those attending will be using phones or tablets to participate in the session. The mobile interface is almost always different, so it is especially useful to see the differences for yourself.

Another leading practice is to team up with colleagues to see what it is like for you to provide direction and guidance to attendees. It's important to experience for yourself what it looks and feels like when other people begin to join your session. What icons appear next to their names and how can you tell if they are on the audio yet? What is it like to help them join a session? Can they see what you have shared and click on the chat and whiteboard tools as intended?

In the case of breakout sessions, it is quite difficult to learn to facilitate these without anyone else there to send into the small groups. In fact, ask colleagues and friends to join from remote locations and connect to the audio when practicing breakouts. This will provide the best and most realistic practice environment as it mimics what it will really be like with a live audience. Remember to have the second computer at your desk so you can see the pop-up messages each participant receives when breakouts are launched.

Using the ACT process (access, click, and team up) will help guide you through learning any new online meeting platform.

Conclusion

Now that we have identified and analyzed the two platform archetypes and a process for learning how to use them, let's consider all the platform features one by one. Both Builders and Revealers generally have the same features, such as screen sharing, chat, annotating, polling, and breakout rooms. What exactly are all these features and how can they be used to create an engaging and effective live online session?

Reflection Questions

- ▸ Which type of platform do you have, a Revealer or a Builder?
- ▸ Have you attended live online sessions in both types? If so, which one do you prefer and why?
- ▸ How will joining a second computer as an attendee help you better deliver your online sessions?

Virtual Platform Roles and In-Session Features

In This Chapter

○ An in-session features checklist for quick reference and guidance when learning the options in your web conferencing platform

○ A breakdown of the roles and how they differ from one another to learn how to best manage your platform

○ A description of each feature complete with stories and examples to further your understanding of how best to use them

One of the most engaging training sessions I facilitate is packed full of practice teach-back activities for my virtual trainers. The session requires me and my producer to use as many of the features of the web conferencing platform as we can. Here is how we do it in Zoom: Participants come to the session having prepared a few slides from which they will teach a lesson of their choice. They share their screen, displaying their prepared content, and then use annotation tools, chat, webcam, audio, and sometimes polling to deliver their segment. Due to the time it takes to let each person teach, my producer and I split them up into two breakout groups, each of us taking the lead on coaching one. My producer works at a fast pace setting up the groups and making sure we all join them properly. I too need to demonstrate my own production skills by assisting each of the participants to take their turn sharing and using all the tools themselves. All of this requires a deep understanding of the platform features to not only use them to lead the class, but to guide others to use each of them too.

How does one go about getting to this level of skill and confidence? It takes knowledge, practice, patience, and perseverance. It begins by examining all the features, so you know what is possible.

There are more features in a web conferencing platform than people realize. The most-used features are audio, webcam, chat, and screen sharing a presentation. Examining the many options available will help engage participants with the delivery of the content. The proper use of these features is best produced by understanding what features are available, how each functions, and how they are used to run meetings, webinars, and virtual classroom training sessions. The platforms have many features in common, though some may lack one or two, or refer to the same features by a different name. To learn about the in-session features of your platform, use this chapter to identify exactly what your platform has and does not have, as well as ideas on how each of the features can be used to deliver your sessions.

Remember, features themselves do not create engagement. It is how they are used that makes the difference!

Table 4-1 is an inventory of in-session features common to most platforms. It's important to know what to look for, so use this as a checklist to identify which features your platform includes, how each of them functions, and ideas on how best to use and support them. Use this resource for quick reference when learning the in-session features of your platform.

Table 4-1. In-Session Features Checklist

✓	Feature	Description
Get Started		
	Roles	The function or part assigned to a person participating in a live online session, determining their level of control and access.
	Audio	Connection to the broadcast, teleconference, or computer audio to hear and speak in a live online session.
	Participant List (including Attention Tracking)	The list of participants, attendees, speakers, panelists, presenters, and hosts participating in the live online session.
	Webcam	A combination of the words "web" and "camera," this feature enables a live video feed using a camera from a computer.
	Recording	An archive of a session for playback later, including the visuals, communications, interactions, and audio.
Basic Interaction		
	Feedback	The buttons or icons that allow participants to indicate status, such as "raise hand," "green check," and "away."
	Chat	A designated area for typing publicly shared and private messages for dialogue, questions, and comments.
	Whiteboard	Noun: a blank space replicating a sheet of paper for online collaboration using annotation tools. Verb: the act of using the annotation tools on the blank space or on top of a shared file or screen.
	Annotation	The typing, writing, and drawing tools located on a designated toolbar to be used to markup shared files and whiteboards.
	Share File	A feature that permits uploading of files into the main meeting room environment, instead of sharing the them via a computer screen or application.
	Share Screen	A feature where the presenter of a live online session shares their computer screen with attendees who can then view programs, applications, files, websites, and so on, directly from the presenter's computer.
Advanced Interaction		
	Polling	A tool used to formally survey an audience where results can be broadcasted and saved.
	Notes	A designated area for notes to be taken, displayed, saved, and shared.

Table 4-1. In-Session Features Checklist (cont.)

Advanced Interaction		
	Q&A	A space designated for formal management of questions and answers.
	File Transfer	A quick way to make files for participants available for download from within the session.
	Breakout	A tool to allow participants to work together in small groups and on shared audio, sharing files, screens, whiteboards, webcams, and other features to collaborate.

In the rest of the chapter you'll find definitions, descriptions with details, and notes for things to be aware of when running online sessions. To ease your introduction to the many features available, I've grouped them into three categories: get started, basic interactions, and advanced interactions.

Get Started Features

The "get started" features include roles, audio, participant panel, webcam, and recording.

Roles

The function or part assigned to a person participating in a live online session, determining their level of control and access.

Each platform has its own terminology for identifying who has control of a session, who can present during one, and what attendees can do when they participate. (If only all the live online platforms used the same terminology, this would make understanding and remembering the content of this section much easier.) Clearly identifying the roles defined in your technology will lay the groundwork for not only how the entire program functions, but also why it works as it does. Here is a list of the most common titles for roles and their function within the platform:

- **Participants:** This is a term used for all roles who have joined a session. It includes the leaders as well as all the attendees. It is often the title of the panel, pod, or pane listing everyone connected.
- **Host, organizer, or moderator:** This role has the login to the site and is responsible for scheduling, editing, starting, and ending the sessions. They also lead on sending invites or obtaining the links

and details to be shared with attendees so they can join the session. The person in this role needs to start the session and maintain their connection to it so attendees can join and participate throughout. They are also typically responsible for recording, changing layouts, and sometimes setting up and launching breakout sessions. The host login is the one with access to all the administrative features available with the account as well. Without a host account, which is connected to the licensing and payment for the use of the technology, a session cannot be run. Some platforms (like Adobe Connect) allow for more than one host to be in a session, while others (like Webex) allow only one at a time, and others (like Zoom) allow co-hosts.

- **Alternate host, organizer, or moderator:** Some platforms allow for alternate hosts to be assigned, enabling one host to set up the sessions, and another to log in on the day of the session to manage it.
- **Presenter:** This is the role controlling what is being shared with the audience at any given moment. The presenter shares their screen to websites and software applications and moves slides that are loaded into the environment. Some platforms allow for more than one presenter; others only permit one at a time. This role can generally be passed from person to person, allowing guest speakers to join sessions without having to own a host account to do so.
- **Panelist:** Some platforms may have a third role to assist with the live delivery of a session. Webex has this role in its Event and Training Center products. A panelist has more privileges in the session than the attendees, but not as much as a presenter or a host. The panelist is usually managing the questions and answers and assisting with monitoring chat messages. It is a way to add more assistants to a large session when a host and presenter are not enough.
- **Attendee:** This is the role assigned to those who have joined the session to attend rather than to lead. They are sometimes also labeled participants in some platforms, though in other platforms participants means everyone, including the leaders, as mentioned earlier. Attendee screens are usually connected to the presenter and the content that they are sharing at any given moment.

A tip to help you learn the different roles: Join a second computer as an attendee to all live online sessions you are hosting. This will immediately inform you of the differences between the roles.

Audio

The connection to the broadcast, teleconference, or computer audio to hear and speak in a live online session.

Managing audio connections is on the top of the list of production tasks and one of the most important aspects of a live online session. And it is often the most common area for technical issues to occur since it can work in many ways, requiring specific technical details for each.

There are three basic requirements for any audio connection to be engaging: the proper audio equipment for sending and receiving sound, a high-speed internet connection, and a quiet location free from background noise. Encourage all who intend to speak in the session to join from a quiet and comfortable place and use a high-speed internet connection. It is also necessary to have a clearly audible line; a high-quality headset, microphone, headphones; and the expertise to control muting and unmuting. Technical interference like disconnected audio due to a poor internet connections, echoes or feedback due to the improper setup of audio, and background noise desperately interfere with online sessions and are frankly unacceptable. Attendees will exit a session that is not comfortable to listen to.

Attendees always need help understanding how to connect to and maintain audio. Send them the instructions in advance and be prepared to share the same information on the screen once they join. Stay alert throughout the session, ready to offer support should disconnections occur.

Of note: If you have participants who are hearing impaired attending your sessions, be sure to follow the organization's expectations and guidelines for supporting their experience. Check with the platform provider to see how features like closed captioning and webcams are used to create an engaging experience for everyone to effectively participate.

There are three types of audio connections for live online sessions: broadcast, teleconference, and computer audio. Let's review a description of each and important details for producing an online session.

Broadcast

An audio broadcast is typically used for large online sessions where attendees are not expected to be speaking; they are listening in as the speakers present. Attendees must first join the session using the recommended internet connection speed and have the proper sound hardware on their devices to hear the presenters through their speakers.

Teleconference

A teleconference is a telephone meeting among two or more participants involving technology more robust than a two-way phone connection. It has multiple dial-in connections and usually supports some form of subconferencing, enabling audio participants to speak together in small groups, separate from the main call. Teleconference numbers can be integrated with the web conferencing system in a variety of ways and are sometimes provided by the platform itself, or by third-party telecom companies. Check the host profile to confirm the type of teleconference connection options included with your account. It may need to be set up in an audio profile, requiring you to enter your teleconference account information, or it may be a choice from a drop-down list when scheduling a session.

Other details to consider with teleconferencing include whether participants must dial in to the call, or if they can enter their phone number to receive a call back. If they must dial in, they need to know which number to call and what codes to enter. If they receive a call back, they must enter a direct phone number for it work as it is usually an automated call that requires buttons to be pressed upon joining. If the call goes to a person at a front desk, they may hang up on it. If it calls and gets another automated system, then the two automated systems won't usually communicate with one another and the call will drop. Your account will determine what is available, and your participants need to know what to do once they join the session. Typically, the teleconference instructions will appear in a pop-up window once a participant joins the session. It is up to them to then follow the instructions on the screen. They often close this and ask for help from the producers of the session, so be prepared for this and ready to assist.

For my collaborative meetings and virtual training sessions where I expect people to actively participate, rather than sending the teleconference numbers in an email in advance, I inform participants that the numbers will appear on their screens after they join with their computers. This is my practice for getting people to resist "just calling into" my session. If I am presenting a webinar where people do not need to collaborate, then this is not necessary because listening in would be an acceptable way to attend.

Computer Audio

This audio is being sent via one's internet connection rather than via a teleconference. It is also sometimes referred to as VoIP (Voice over Internet Protocol). This audio will be heard from the computer or device speakers used to join the online session. Strong internet connections are key to this type of audio connection working seamlessly as it can sometimes be choppy. Some platforms are better than others at providing clear and effective computer audio, so it is important to test in advance. It is also a leading practice to always use some form of a headset, headphones, or pods when using computer audio.

In addition to the different ways to connect audio, you should be aware of enabling or disabling participants' microphones. Some systems allow you to enable all participants' microphones at once, while others require participants to raise their hands to speak. Either way, explore how participants can connect their computer audio, and what settings need to be adjusted so they can speak if called upon to do so. Encourage people to connect early or in an advance session if using computer audio is new. Many struggle to not only connect to it, but to understand how it works in the first place, so do not assume they will figure it out on their own and know what to do the day of the session.

Whether using teleconferencing or computer audio, it is necessary to understand the controls for quieting the audio connection. What can the host control, and what do the participants need to know? Most audio connections have an option for a host to mute all lines. For a teleconference, this is typically accessed by pressing numbers on the phone, or if computer audio is integrated with the platform, it will be a menu option in the interface. There is also usually a setting for teleconference attendees to be muted upon entry; in the case of computer audio it can be set so that participants cannot enable their microphones until permitted. These options are mostly used for large online sessions and webinars where attendees do not need to speak.

Individual lines can also be muted and unmuted, and this can be done by the host, the presenter, and if enabled, the participants themselves. With integrated audio, these options are usually accessed in menus, on toolbars, or sometimes by right-clicking. Teleconferencing options usually have command controls for hosts and participants alike to press buttons on their phones to mute and unmute.

Additionally, most platforms have visual indicators of audio connections such as red lines when people are muted and moving icons when people are speaking. The indicators work only when attendees have properly connected to the audio. For example, when using a teleconference, participants may not notice or follow the prompts for attendee codes, and they skip entering them. This is seen in Webex when there is a list of call-in users on the participants panel, and in Adobe Connect and in Zoom where phone numbers get listed separately from the attendees' names. The solution to this is different for each platform—in Webex they must hang up, call in again, and enter their attendee ID number; in Adobe Connect the host can merge the listed phone number with the attendee name; and in Zoom attendees can press #, participant ID, # if they skipped it in the first place—so take note of these details and teach participants to do the same.

When I'm leading a virtual event, I only control muting when I am in a large online session or webinar. In my virtual classrooms and online meetings, I teach participants to mute and unmute themselves once they have connected their audio. The more that people know how to do technical things for themselves, the better they are at participating properly in live online sessions moving forward!

Lastly, I'm frequently asked what equipment I recommend and as of the writing of this book, I use a simple, inexpensive, yet high-quality USB Logitech headset to present via computer audio. I sometimes use AirPods when presenting from a teleconference, and I use a Plantronics telephone headset when I present from a landline. Earbuds continue to improve and are becoming increasingly more effective as well as comfortable. The important thing is to test your equipment in advance to ensure it is clear and comfortable.

Participant Panel, Pane, or Pod

This is the list of participants, attendees, speakers, panelists, presenters, and hosts participating in the live online session.

The area with a list of all participants in the session indicates who is online, how their audio is connected, and what feedback they are providing throughout the session. The list is always visible to the host of a session, and in most platforms can be set to allow all participants to see one another too. Check meeting settings and participant privileges to adjust what everyone can see and to decide what is best for your session. In general, meetings and training sessions where participants need to collaborate usually show the participant list, and webinars and other types of large sessions where the presentation and information sharing is the focus do not.

The participant list provides insight not only into who is connected, but also how they are connected. For example, someone who has joined from the mobile application using their tablet or mobile phone will often be indicated by a special icon to alert hosts. Pay attention to this indicator as the mobile device interface is often visually different and sometimes limited in features.

Another indication from the participant list will be how participants have connected their audio. Look for phone icons for teleconference, and headset or microphone icons for computer audio. These same icons will show whether participants are muted, and others will move when the participant speaks, or a sound can be heard coming from their connection. Other indicators might include one for the strength of someone's internet connection, or whether their screen is active at each moment, sometimes referred to as attention tracking or an engagement meter. This is not actually tracking their attention levels; it's indicating whether the window they are using for their connection to the platform is active or not.

In short, analyzing the participant list and paying close attention to all that it has to offer is an excellent way to look for nonverbal communication cues in a live online session.

You might be surprised to hear this, but I often focus more on the participant list than my slides to engage an audience! I look at the list for feedback, and I use attendees' names often and regularly, because as Dale Carnegie famously said, their names are to each of them "the sweetest, most important sound in any language."

Webcam

A combination of the words "web" and "camera," the webcam feature enables a live video feed using a camera from a computer.

In recent years, appearing on a webcam has become increasingly more popular and accepted in online sessions. Seeing one another can truly personalize an online experience and help to engage an audience that otherwise might be inclined to check out. In the past, two common reasons (I think of them as excuses) were used for not using this simple and effective feature: weak internet connections affecting session performance, and a general fear of or lack of comfort being on camera. After all, not all of us signed up to be television broadcasters when we became online presenters or were asked to do our training sessions using web conferencing platforms! The technology has come a long way though, thanks to stronger internet connections and streamlined platforms with high performance capabilities. So, it is natural that webcams are now more acceptable than they were in the beginning.

Webcams usually reside in the same area in the session as the participant list. Some platforms make webcams the focus, while others allow placement where the presenter chooses. The options usually allow for hosts to decide who can use webcams (such as only the presenter or everyone), as well as setting webcams to default to on or off upon joining the session. You can also set the view: alternating in and out of full screen, viewing only the person speaking, or viewing many participants at once. It is generally true that the more webcams that are turned on for a session, the more internet bandwidth is required to keep them streaming in real time.

Webcams work well for introductions or any time that seeing a person or an object would be helpful for learning to occur. For example, I once learned how to connect and set up my home office Cisco VoIP phone from the online training our IT department ran using Webex. The trainer used the webcam the entire time because he had it set to zoom in on the phone itself while I was working on my phone at the same time. It was a simple yet effective use of the webcam!

People typically enjoy seeing one another in meetings, and for webinars and virtual classroom sessions they especially appreciate meeting their presenters and trainers. It is important to be aware of how you look on webcam as well as your lighting and background. Here are some leading practices for looking great on webcam each time:

- **Lighting:** Pay attention to your lighting by having a light that brightens your face. Avoid being lit from the side or from behind, like from a window.
- **Angle:** Set the angle of the camera to be at your eye level and watch out for angles in the room that show lines in awkward places.
- **Background:** Ensure the background is free from distractions and complementary to your brand, your messaging, and your organization's culture.
- **Equipment:** Consider using a better webcam than the one built into your computer. You'll experience better image quality with additional options for settings.
- **Smile:** Be sure your face is centered, look directly into the camera when speaking, and don't forget to smile!

I have long referred to and appreciate the tips and advice Caleb Wojcik offers on his site. Refer to his blog post for more information as well as ideas on the best equipment to use, not only for webcams, but for all your video creation needs: calebwojcik.com/blog/10-ways-to-look-better-on-a-webcam.

Recording

A recording is an archive of a session for playback later, including the visuals, communications, interactions, and audio.

Recordings of webinars, virtual classroom sessions, and some meetings can be a useful resource for capturing specific moments in time that are not easily repeated (such as if a guest speaker has been invited for a special presentation). If participants need to exit a training session early, they can watch what they have missed. Other uses for a recording would be to track for consistency, compliance needs, and even training other trainers.

The recording feature of a web conferencing platform typically captures both the audio and visual aspects of a session, creating a video file that's available for playback. The type of video file created is determined by your platform and range from propriety formats to standard .mov and .mp4 files. It is important to confirm that the audio of your session is also included with your recording, and whether there are any special settings required to make it work properly. Most platforms will include broadcast and computer audio, but depending on how a teleconference is connected to your session, additional settings may be necessary.

Once a recording has been made, it then gets stored to a designated location. Some platforms require you to save your recording locally and then you can upload or share it as you see fit. Other platforms allow your host account to store the recording file on their servers, designating a set amount of space per host account. Once the recording is stored, a link will often be generated, which then can be shared with participants. Some platforms even have a way for participants to be invited to view the recording.

When it comes to virtual training, do not mistake the recordings of interactive virtual classroom sessions as a replacement for the learning session. Because it does not replicate the live interaction, a recording will not influence learning in the same way it did for those who participated. Also, most people won't watch a recording for more than 10 minutes, so they are likely to miss out on a lot of it anyway.

Basic Interaction Features

The basic interaction features include feedback, chat, whiteboard, annotation, share file, and share screen.

Feedback

The feedback buttons or icons allow participants to indicate status, such as "raise hand," "green check," "away," and many more options.

The feedback icons, typically located near the list of participants, are a simple and highly effective way to check engagement levels with live online attendees. Virtual feedback replicates the type of nonverbal communication that participants provide during in-person sessions when raising their hands and nodding in agreement. It's obvious when a person steps away from a session in person, but in a webinar it can easily go unnoticed.

I encourage attendees to click the green check or thumbs up icons any time they are nodding their head in agreement, or to choose an emoji when they smile or feel confused. I also use the yes and no indicators to conduct instant feedback polls. It is unnecessary and time consuming to launch a formal poll for a simple yes or no response. I also request attendees mark themselves away any time they are not available. This helps to avoid the awkward silence when someone calls on them and there is no answer.

Using the feedback tools helps attendees learn to be more accountable for their own live online experiences. Here are some more of my favorite verbal examples of requesting attendees to use the feedback tools in a live session:

- Please click the green checkmark if this example resonates with you and the red x if does not.
- Let's applaud your colleagues' efforts! Click the applause button or send an applause emoticon in chat.
- Please mark "away" or use the "coffee mug" if you need to step out.
- Let's click on the green checkmarks to indicate we have returned from the breakout and are ready to debrief.
- I've noticed a few of you have requested I slow down the review of the process. Thank you for indicating this using your feedback.

Note that every platform has different feedback icons. Webex Training and Event Centers have more feedback options than Webex Meeting Center, which only has a raised hand option. Adobe Connect and Zoom have quite a few to choose from, but they are in different locations. Skype for Business does not have them, but there are many icons to choose to send using the chat.

I prefer platforms that have a toolbar with at least a few feedback icons to choose from, that all participants can see what they and others display, and that appears next to each participant name for quick reference. This helps me gauge levels of participation and provides participants with another simple way to communicate while live online.

It is also important to check what participants can see and when they can see it. For example, in Webex Meeting Center, the host and presenter can see an attendee's raised hand, but other participants cannot. And in Zoom, the nonverbal feedback options are not in the meeting until the meeting host enables that feature in their profile's meeting settings. Explore the options in the settings on the host profile as well as inside the meeting once it has been started. Most platforms include some form of visual or nonverbal feedback as described, but some do require they be enabled before they can be used.

Chat

Chat is a designated area for typing publicly shared and private messages for dialogue, questions, and comments.

Chat is one of the main methods of communication in live online sessions, and often the first area where you can provide production support once a participant has joined. Do not underestimate the power of this simple tool as it can be one of the best methods of communication available. It's easily found in most platforms and commonly used in not only webinars and online meetings, but also in day-to-day communications with many applications and mobile devices.

Use chat for commentary, questions, and conversations. Go beyond telling people to "use chat if they want," and instead require it as a regular way of reacting to the interactions throughout. For example, encourage conversations among participants, otherwise known as "chatversations" (LaBorie and Stone 2015). Show images and have participants respond in chat. React to what they send verbally, as if it were said over the audio. Send links through chat to instantly provide online resources to participants. View it as a conversation and watch personal connections to your participants increase, making the session no longer feel like a one-way presentation.

Figure 4-1 is an example of a chatversation that occurred during one of my train-the-virtual-trainer workshops. We were debriefing the effectiveness of a learning activity that uses images to help participants make connections. Note the comments at the end of the exchange, where participants are chatting amongst themselves, learning from the ideas that each is sharing. Presenters, trainers, meeting leaders, and producers alike should support an environment that allows chatversations such as the illustrated example to flourish.

Chat is typically easy to locate in each platform and rarely do participants need training on how to use it. Not all platforms show the chat by default, so look on the toolbars to see if it can be expanded. Be sure to keep the chat in view always, especially if webcams are not being used by the attendees. If the chat panel is in the way, it can often be minimized or resized and usually has a flashing indicator once a new message has arrived.

Figure 4-1. Chatversation Example

Sonia: I love the description you provided Mary Lynn!
Sonia: Kelly is the most FLUID people I know!
Kelly: Thanks?
Sonia: YES!
Marion: LOVE IT
Melissa: great exercise
Staci: Helping to get more familiar with tools.
Mary: very good activity
Melissa: hard to decide so many great pictures :)
Kelly: everyone's learning technically, and it gives people time to think
Marion: Great idea to use inspiring visuals. Good that they are numbered
Sonia: This is great b/c it not only gives a visual representation but engaging them on the phone too.
Mary: gets people thinking
Sonia: EXCELLENT Melissa!
Mary-Lynn: It gets people thinking about a topic without saying, "think about …
Kelly: I agree!
Sonia: If you have a large group it might be hard to get through everyone.
Mary-Lynn: Engages right brain
Sonia: That's great Mary Lynn! I didn't even think of that. It helps people get into that creative learning mode!

Chat usually has settings for participants to send both public and private messages. If you are running a sales and marketing webinar, it may be useful to hide a chat that the entire audience may view. Conversely, in a small group team meeting or a training session, an open chat is helpful for commentary and collaboration. Check your platform's default settings to confirm where it begins, and then check the in-session settings or attendee privileges to see what can be altered as needed. Two additional questions to answer regarding how chat works in your platform:

- Can the chat file be saved? This is helpful for keeping records and referring to anything that may be needed following the session.
- Can the hosts view private chats between attendees? If private chat messages are allowed to occur between participants, does the host have access to these? If so, consider letting participants know this is the case as they may not be aware.

Whiteboard

Noun: A blank space replicating a sheet of paper for online collaboration using annotation tools.
Verb: The act of using the annotation tools on the blank space or on top of a shared file or screen.

A whiteboard is a powerful collaboration tool more commonly used in online meetings and virtual classroom sessions than in large webinars. It replicates the type of activities done on an easel flipchart, or a wall-mounted dry erase board: brainstorming, note taking, diagramming, and the like. Most web conferencing platforms have a formal whiteboard that can be shared, as well as ways to enable annotation tools so that shared content can be whiteboarded or annotated upon. (Referring to the latter is what makes whiteboard not only a noun but also a verb, for example, to whiteboard upon a slide.)

One of my favorite and most effective uses of a blank whiteboard is for a partnered listening skills activity. Two people are sent into a breakout room to practice their listening and communication skills. One person is given a picture to describe to the other person who must draw it on the whiteboard. They then compare notes and debrief how well they described the picture and asked clarifying questions. It is always a highly engaging activity. Figure 4-2 is from a program where eight teams of two participated and then shared their work.

Figure 4-2. Breakout Whiteboard Activity Example

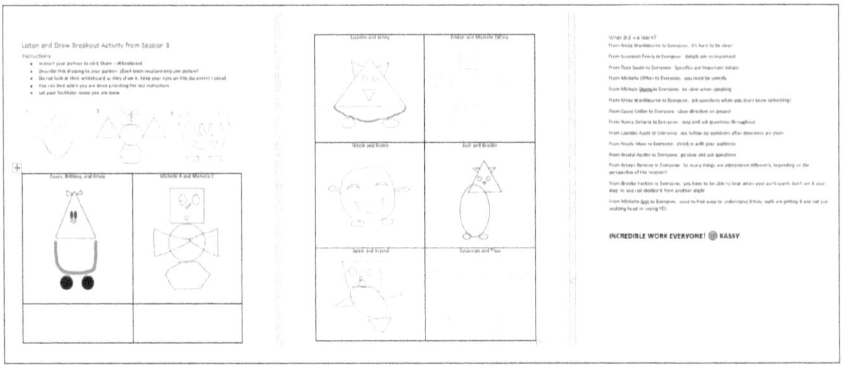

Annotation

The typing, writing, and drawing tools located on a designated toolbar to be used to markup shared files and whiteboards.

When using *whiteboarding* as a verb, it is important to know about the annotation feature. The platform's annotation tools allow a whiteboard and other files and shared screens to be written or drawn upon. Annotation tools are usually available to leaders, hosts, and presenters of sessions. They are needed for any of the techniques listed in the whiteboard section of this chapter to be used by participants of the session, and they will typically need to be enabled for them. Look in the attendee privileges options of your platform to enable these tools and then teach participants how to use them during opening activities.

Annotating or whiteboarding answers and ideas is one of the most effective ways to gauge participation levels. It not only provides immediate responses, but it is also easy to save results and refer to them later. Be sure to investigate where to activate the annotation tools for participants as some platforms allow it at an administrative level, and others require it be done once the session has started. Enable the annotation privileges to allow participants to collaborate and write their ideas and comments on shared files and actual whiteboards.

Some specific functional questions to research within your platform include:

- Who can share whiteboards?
- Can slides and files function as whiteboards by permitting annotation to occur on top of them?
- Can the annotations be edited, moved, copied, or deleted?
- If not annotating on slides and files, how many whiteboards can be added and where do they display?
- Can additional pages be added to a shared whiteboard?
- Can the annotations be saved? If so, how and where are they stored?

Here are a few leading practices and ideas for successful whiteboard usage:

- Have participants place a pointer or type their initials on the whiteboard space prior to typing a response. This is called "claiming their real estate" and will keep them from typing over one another.

- Create a table or a grid to organize the space on your shared file that will be whiteboarded or annotated upon. Prepopulate participants names in each area.
- Add images to a slide and let participants use their annotation tools to make notes, draw connections, or add reactions.

In most cases I prefer to use slides with space for participants to annotate upon rather than using a blank whiteboard. Providing directions, images, and designated spaces to type makes the activity clear for participants.

I do use blank whiteboards in meetings for spontaneous collaboration, or sometimes in breakout activities when participants are assigned to create a drawing or map a process. But participants do need to know how to share their whiteboards, and that is not always where I want to spend time. I'd rather they focus on the point of the learning activity rather than getting confused by the technical steps of presenting in the platform.

Share File (Upload)

A feature that permits uploading of files into the main meeting room environment, instead of sharing them via a computer screen or application share.

Uploading files into designated areas in your web conferencing platform (such as a share pod in Adobe Connect, or the main content window in Webex) gives the presenter the advantage of privacy during live delivery. This is an alternative to sharing one's screen to display the files through their source applications where all the toolbars and buttons from the applications are seen. Uploading a file is like printing a copy and distributing it to the audience. This feature is not available in all platforms, and it is one of the primary differences between a Builder platform and a Revealer (see chapter 3).

Another advantage to uploading files into the shared environment is that it allows a presenter, should they choose, to plan ahead by placing the intended files into the environment before the scheduled time of the presentation. It also sometimes makes navigating the environment simpler because the extra tools inside the source application are not shown, permitting the focus to be on the tools of the web conferencing platform like chat and feedback instead.

Shared files that are prepared for interaction with enough blank space for whiteboarding answers to questions, thoughts, and ideas are an effective way to engage participants. Files can often be annotated upon for increased interaction and engaging activities like those mentioned in the whiteboard-ing and annotation sections. Develop slides and files to be uploaded in this way if it is possible, so they become a working space for collaboration rather than just a presentation.

Figure 4-3 is an example of a prepared PowerPoint slide that has been shared and annotated upon. Note the blank space and the rows so participants have enough space to type and share ideas.

Figure 4-3. Share File Example

	NAME	LEARNED?	IMPACT?
What have you learned?	Raghu	Create content that draws the participants	Helps engagement and learning
	Bill	Lot's of great new ideas	Continuous Improvement
	Paul	I can do this	I will do this
What will be the impact?	Carol	I learned the most from being a participant, evaluating how things	I can do this! Many of the classes I teach will work this way
	celeste	practice, get feedback, there is so much more to do than I thought was	Much more willing to try some online learning.
	Janine	Zoom features and getting more familiar with it, getting opportunity as a participant to see what works and what doesn't, the feedback received	Keep practicing to improve delivery of online learning to vastly improve the learning experience for others
	David	Be patient/practice/get feedback	Ability to convert live learning programs to help more people.
	Rod	So much. Technology, techniques, tips, tricks, timing...	I am confident this is where we're going, and confident that I can be a part of it, thanks!
p.32 DOCUMENT YOUR ACTION PLAN	Michael	KISS: Keep It Simple & Straightforward i.e., slides, instructions, exercises	READY TO PLAY!

Share Screen

A feature where the presenter of a live online session shares their computer screen with attendees who can then view programs, applications, files, and websites directly from the presenter's computer.

Software and systems training sessions are often conducted using desk-top, application, or web sharing. When a presenter shares their screen, it allows attendees to view the entire desktop, one application at a time, or even a web page depending on what the presenter decides to share. The person presenting controls the navigation of the screen while the participants follow along. It is like asking a group of people to gather around your computer while you show them something. Your hands are on your computer, while they watch and observe.

Most web conferencing platforms have this feature, and as described in chapter 3, this is the primary way to share content in the Revealer platform types. It is the presenter's choice how much to share: desktop or screen share is showing everything on that computer screen, application share will only show the applications that are selected, and web browser share is just a shortcut for application share of one's browser. Many platforms also allow for portions of a screen to be shared so a presenter has the option to indicate exactly what is seen. Additionally, most platforms include a way to "pause" the screen share to take a break or to open or refer to something unnecessary for the audience to see at that time. A second computer joined as an attendee will provide a proper view of exactly what you are sharing, so I advise you do this when you are presenting and using screen share.

Of note is that attendees do not need to have any of the applications being shared by the presenter installed on their own computers, making this a powerful feature for web conferencing systems. It is also important to remember that participants see the mouse, the toolbars, and all the windows when desktop sharing. This includes any pop-up windows like email reminders or instant messages received during the presentation, so it is best to close unused applications, and disable pop ups while in a live session.

A subfeature of screen share is remote control. Some platforms allow presenters to offer participants remote control of their shared desktop or applications. If a presenter chooses to use this feature, it is given to one participant at a time. In most cases, a participant accepts the offer of control by clicking on their own view of the shared screen and navigating what they see at the lead of the presenter.

An example of this in a virtual training or sales demonstration is when the presenter wants to let an attendee use the application that is being shared from the presenter's computer. Software salespeople love this feature because it lets prospective buyers try using the software before the prospect has access to it. Trainers use it as an interactive, hands-on learning technique when performing a software training demonstration.

Remote control is most often used in technical support sessions where an IT professional asks permission to remotely access your computer. You would present your desktop and then offer the remote control to the IT professional who would then proceed to click the screen to troubleshoot your problem.

Sometimes remote control is used in training to allow participants to take turns practicing navigating a software system, and sometimes salespeople use it during a demonstration to give the prospects an opportunity to see what it is truly like to use the systems they are selling.

Advanced Interaction Features

The advanced interaction features include polling, notes, Q&A, file transfer, and breakout.

Polling

A tool used to formally survey an audience where results can be broadcasted and saved.

Polling is a popular and easy feature to efficiently check in with and engage an online audience. You can prepare questions with multiple-choice answers in advance of the virtual session. Or, depending on the platform, you may be able to create polls in the meetings themselves, which can be saved, launched, and even reused in other meetings in the future to collect new results with a new audience.

A particularly engaging use of polling is to create a quiz to break up a lecture. During a training on a complex software application, for example, the trainer can pause at specific moments to launch a multiple-choice, single answer poll. This engaging use of polling serves as a form of knowledge check, giving each participant a moment to stop and think about what had just been covered.

Many platforms have sections of the company's branded site where polls can be created and attached to sessions. Zoom, for example, allows hosts to create polls once a session is scheduled by just editing the session and scrolling down to the "add poll" section at the bottom of the page. GoToWebinar has a polling section on the hosts' login, where polls can be created ahead of time and attached to as many sessions as needed.

Additionally, most platforms allow polls to be created in the meetings themselves, saved, launched, and even reused in other meetings in the future to collect new results with a different audience. Webex Training Center has a poll questionnaire editor that can be downloaded from the company's branded Webex site and used to create polling files ahead of time, with the polls then available for use in any Webex meeting as needed. They are saved as files with an .atp extension and need to be saved with all the other session files planned for the delivery. Create the polling files in advance if possible and use them repeatedly in your live online sessions. Determine whether the polls or polling files your host login creates can be shared with other hosts for use their own sessions.

When creating the polling files or questions, see if they can include one question or many on the same file or survey. Also determine if your questions can be multiple-choice (radio-buttons where respondents can choose one answer from a list), multiple answer (check boxes where respondents can choose many answers from a list), or short answer (a space for respondents to type their own words).

Remember to respond appropriately to the answers and build your comments and discussion into the session experience. Some presenters will run polls as a form of engagement and interaction, but then fail to thoughtfully comment on the answers provided. When using polling, create a slide with the question on it or some other visual connected to the question. This serves as a reminder to not only run the poll as part of the production tasks, but also provides a reason to verbally set up the question being asked. Guide attendees in how to respond technically, indicating where the poll question will appear, and then be purposefully silent while they read and select their answers. Once they have responded, let them know you are about to reveal the results, if appropriate, and share with them why you asked the question and how it is connected to the purpose of the presentation or training. Avoid polling just to "have interaction"—doing so is not engaging. Use it to help attendees connect to the meaning of the presentation and to allow the presenter to gain insight into what the audience is thinking.

Notes

A designated area for notes to be taken, displayed, saved, and shared.

Many platforms include a designated panel, pod, or pane for notes to be taken and sometimes shared during a session. Some platforms like Webex Meeting Center default to allowing each attendee to privately use a notes panel. These notes are saved once the attendee exits the meeting. Alternatively, Webex hosts may change this setting to instead designate a single note taker who can display their notes throughout the meeting, save a copy of the file, and distribute them following the session.

Adobe Connect has a notes pod that can be used in any layout. The settings can be adjusted to allow attendees to add notes, but it is mostly used for presenters to share prepared notes for viewing while they are leading their sessions. Common examples are websites, references, or instructions.

Determine if your platform includes this feature, and then decide if a note taker is required, and if this is a place for attendees to take their own notes, or a place for shared notes to be displayed.

Q&A

A space designated for formal management of questions and answers.

Attendees of webinars and virtual classroom training sessions will have questions, and depending on the number of participants, it can be challenging to keep track of them. Session leaders can benefit from an organized way for questions to be submitted in a live session. This is particularly useful in large webinars where many questions can come in at once. It's easy to miss them and to run out of time to answer each one. A formal Q&A panel, pod, or pane organizes the questions, indicating who sent each one and at what time. It will also often indicate whether it was responded to and who answered it. Q&A provides an archive of all the questions and answers, permitting the session leaders to save a file and follow up as necessary.

Q&A is typically set up so that questions are privately sent to the hosts, organizers, presenters, and panelists. Other attendees do not usually see the questions at the time they are sent in, but session leaders have the choice to respond privately or to reveal the question and their accompanying answer publicly. GoToWebinar has a Q&A panel for attendees instead of a chat panel. This platform is designed for large audiences, so while the session leaders may send chat messages, attendees may only use the Q&A panel to submit text communications. Be certain to promote your webinar assistants to the role of host, co-organizer, panelist, or other leader role necessary so they can help manage the questions throughout the session.

On several occasions I have had over a thousand participants in a webinar I was presenting. Every time I have been a part of such a large webinar, I have had more than one producer helping to manage it and assisting with questions. Using chat to capture questions is risky because it is easy to miss them in the flow of all the other comments. The designated Q&A feature keeps all questions in one place, allowing those assisting to manage them, share them over the audio with the presenter, save them for later, dismiss ones that aren't relevant, and so on. Saving them for later without having to sort through a running chat file is useful and engaging for participants who can then be confident their questions do not get missed.

File Transfer

A quick way to make files for participants available for download from within the session.

The share file feature is for presenting and showing information to attendees. File *transfer* is used when a presenter, meeting host, or trainer wants to give files to attendees to take with them. Handouts and manuals can be easily provided to participants using this File Transfer feature. Most platforms include a way to send files to participants once they have joined the session. It's convenient to make files available in the moment to attendees, especially for those who did not receive them ahead of time. It's also an efficient way to share the results of collaboration during an online meeting. For example, perhaps a team has gathered to review the project plan, making notes and adjustments during the meeting. I have often led meetings sharing my desktop to work on a project plan and make changes. Once the file has been edited, I use file transfer to share the edited file with everyone instead of having to email it to the team.

Each platform works differently so investigate exactly if, where, and how this feature is available. For example, Adobe Connect has a dedicated files pod, Webex has the option to transfer from the file menu, and Zoom makes a button available via the in-meeting chat once it has been enabled in the host's profile. In each case, participants need to be alerted to the availability of the files, otherwise they may go unnoticed. They also need instructions on exactly where the files are located within the session, and what to do to download them for viewing later. It is also important to check if there is a size limit placed upon the files that are being sent using this feature. It can sometimes be a great way to bypass email file size restrictions as these file transfer features often can support larger files.

Breakout

A tool to allow participants to work together in small groups and on shared audio, sharing files, screens, whiteboards, webcams, and other features to collaborate.

A breakout session, or sometimes also called a breakout room, is a functionality in web conferencing platforms that allows hosts to place participants into smaller groups, separate from the main session. The participants are transferred from the main visual and audio connection and placed in a smaller group, where visual and audio is shared only with their group members. Check the audio settings on your platform to ensure sub-conferencing is enabled and ready to support the breakouts.

Once participants have joined the breakout, they can typically use chat, whiteboards, and screen sharing, and in many cases they can also still use their webcams. The audio, if integrated, will automatically transfer to their small group once they join it. Participants can work together, save their work, take notes, and prepare to share their experiences upon their return, if requested. Most platforms have a way for participants to save their work, while many have a way for hosts to do it for them.

Working in small groups with other online participants is an effective and engaging way to apply key lessons from any training session or even a large online conference. Use breakouts for activities like role plays, problem solving, or case studies where teams work together to create solutions, share ideas, and debrief key learning concepts. Always include instructions on not only what they are to do during the breakout, but also technically how the group time will work. For example, I have a final breakout activity that takes about 20 minutes to run for one of my live online workshops. At the end of a session where I have covered an introduction to facilitating and producing in the virtual classroom, I put participants in teams of three to four and give them a list of the top 10 lessons learned about online training to review. These things were generally covered, but not specifically covered as a list of 10, so it is new but related content. It lets them consider the topic that we have discussed and experienced together, but with further insight for their own consideration. I ask them to review the list, choose one item that resonates, and discuss it with each other. It is a thoughtful way to advance their understanding of the content, and a socially collaborative way to wrap up a live online training session.

For breakouts in Builder-type platforms, any instructions or content can be placed in the rooms ahead of time, while for the Revealer-type platforms, it is recommended to send participants the materials in advance of the session, as part of their participant materials. Builder platforms that have this feature allow hosts to prepare breakout rooms that are preloaded with content and assignments in advance of the sessions. Once the session has begun, there will be a way for hosts to determine who should be placed in each room. This is a key differentiator for Builder-type platforms. In contrast, Revealer-type platforms require hosts to launch breakout rooms once the session has started. This requires the host to determine who is going into each room and then to launch the breakout rooms without any content in them. The participants will need to refer to or share their own content once they are connected in their small breakout group.

Hosts, co-hosts, presenters, organizers, and panelists can usually join the various breakout rooms to observe and offer assistance. It's usually not the case that participants can join each other's breakout rooms, but it may be a setting that can be altered if this is needed. Locate the breakout session area of your platform to practice clicking to join and leave the different rooms. Test everything in advance, including the audio connections, with as many participant computers you can locate and convince to join your practice session.

Participants typically have ways to ask for help once they have joined their breakout. This is sometimes in the form of a special area in the chat, or a new dialog box only available in the breakout room. They can click to raise their hands or send messages. Also, hosts usually have a way to broadcast messages to all groups while they are in the breakout rooms, keeping them from having to join each room, one at a time, to send a message. Check the menu options or the options on the breakout panels for ways to communicate with participants once they have joined their breakout room.

Remember, not all platforms have this feature. Check whether your platform does and then recheck the audio settings to ensure that they are compatible with breakouts. This feature takes practice to get comfortable managing. Give yourself time to learn it and to manage the communication with everyone. Additionally, answer the following questions to be completely prepared to support breakout rooms:

- How many breakouts can be created?
- How many people can be in each one?

- How does content get preloaded into the rooms, if working with a Builder-type platform?
- How is content saved and shared?
- How do hosts and other leaders join each of the breakouts if needed?
- How do the attendees indicate they need help?
- How can a broadcast message be sent to the participants in breakout rooms?

For all my breakout activities, I always create a slide with instructions separating activity instructions from technical directions. I also ensure these same details are included in the participant materials for independent reference.

Conclusion

Knowing the features of your web conferencing platform enables you to prepare for an engaging live online experience. It is exciting to know what the system is capable of so that you can connect with your attendees in interactive and collaborative ways, beyond only talking and sharing slides. The focus of the next chapter is putting all these features together with a live audience in attendance—that is, actually producing a live virtual session.

Reflection Questions

▸ What features are you already comfortable using?

▸ Which ones are you most interesting in learning next?

▸ How will you adapt or change the example activities shared in this chapter?

Producing a Virtual Session: Before, During, and After

In This Chapter

- ⬡ Getting ready to produce a live online session, including setting up your workspace for maximum comfort and effectiveness
- ⬡ Detailed checklists for preparing four key areas: technical details, content, presenters, and attendees
- ⬡ A step-by-step guide for producing a live session and a checklist for wrap up tasks

We planned our virtual training session for weeks in advance, setting up our offices and workspaces, preparing the audio and the technology on our computers and devices, and getting the trainers ready to present online, the content ready to be delivered online, and the attendees everything they needed to be successful. Or, at least we thought we had prepared the attendees.

We sent them the equipment they needed, like headsets and system requirements; we made sure they tested their computers and audio ahead of time; we ensured they had all the materials; and we even held live test sessions to help ease them into all of it. We were all set, having prepared every detail for before, during, and the follow-up after the session.

We opened the session early and excitedly waited for everyone to join. And that was when only one of the attendees joined the session and said, "We're here!" Every one of them had gathered into one conference room to sit together for their online class. They were all in one physical space, using one computer and a speaker phone. All the polls, chats, annotated whiteboards, and breakouts we had planned—they could not be done. We had failed to tell them to be at their own desk and using their own computer and audio connections.

We forgot to mention the most basic detail about being online: That being in person together in one room is not an online training. This setup was not going to allow us to use all the features we had planned for a full live online training session. All we could do in this situation was broadcast into their room and lead a training session that was like any other in-person training where they could turn to one another to discuss topics and collaborate on learning activities. It was just us online, with the one attendee computer that had joined as a team of 10 people! We ended up not having much technology to manage at all that day, but we were rather disappointed about it after all that we had prepared for them to do using it.

One of the biggest concerns live online presenters and trainers have is how they will manage all the technical aspects of the webinar, meeting, or virtual classroom session at the same time they need to present the content. It is their first fear, followed closely by learning to engage an audience that is not physically in front of them.

Remember the first time you ever gave a speech, presented at work, or delivered your first training in front of a live audience? I recall this fear of everyone just staring, waiting for me to do something embarrassing. Fast forward to presenting and training online and now we are afraid that we cannot see them! The fear is more about the unknown than anything else.

Whether working with a person in the role of a producer or planning to take care of the production tasks on your own, focus, preparation, patience, and a dash of courage will carry you through the day of the big event. Taking the time to carefully prepare and get all technical, content, presenter, and attendee details in place will make any unexpected moments once the session is live much easier to manage. Having a plan of action, a checklist, some scripting, and a process for managing issues that may arise in the moment will create confidence and a sense of control. And following up with successes, actions, and next steps will solidify the experience, making way for clearer and smoother live online sessions in the future. Let's examine the details for getting ready, going live, and following up with your online sessions.

Getting Ready

In addition to setting up your workspace, pay attention to four key areas—technology, content, presenter, and attendees—and have a backup plan in place for each. Be sure to also review chapters 8 and 9 on how to get participants ready to attend and participate in your live online session, and if working in partnership with another person, how to conduct a rehearsal, dry run, or walk-through once all these details are in place.

Setting Up Your Space

Producing live online sessions from a properly arranged space is as important to your success as your knowledge of the features of the technology. When preparing your office or your desk, be certain it is a comfortable and quiet space from which you can work. Minimize distractions around you and remove background noise. Let others know you are in session by placing a sign on your door. People have even been known to use yellow-and-black caution tape to remind others to be quiet while they are presenting live online.

Look around the space and be sure that what displays on camera is what you want for your presentation. (See chapter 4 for tips on setting up your webcam environment effectively.) Be sure to have comfortable seating that does not make noise or otherwise interfere with your session. Some presenters choose to use a standing desk, allowing them to walk around when they present and to assist with keeping up their energy. If using this style of desk, pay attention to how you are being viewed on webcam as it may be distracting to see someone moving around and possibly going in and out of screen.

Devices

Many people choose to have at least two computers: one to present from and another to join as an attendee. It is increasingly common to have an additional monitor to better view the multiple open documents and the expanded pods or panels from the platform. Others also choose to have more than one type of computer or device join the session, including PCs, Macs, iPads, and other mobile devices. This is necessary if production support will be required for these devices, but if attendees aren't joining from them, then this is likely unnecessary.

I have always used two computers to deliver my sessions, and have recently decided an additional monitor is helpful for expanding my view. It is imperative for me to engage participants in chat and on the participant panel with their feedback, so I find that second monitor is the best place to see those interactions. I don't want to try to float those panels over my slides as I want them to be as large as possible for the best viewing. The second computer is always in the session as an attendee so I can quickly refer to that unique view. To provide accurate and clear instructions, I need this view to be confident in my delivery.

See Figures 5-1 and 5-2 for examples of computer setups.

Figure 5-1. Device Setup #1

Here is a picture of my desk when I am getting ready to teach my live virtual instructor-led sessions. Note there is a cell phone for back up and a Mac to reference the differences in that interface.

Figure 5-2. Device Setup #2

Here is a picture of my producer's desk when we delivered a webinar together. Note he decided to use dual monitors for both computers.

Internet Connection

High-speed internet connections are also a requirement that almost goes without mention. After all, what is a live online meeting, webinar, or virtual training session without the internet? It's just a phone call. It is of the utmost importance to have the highest internet speed available to you when leading a live online session. Check with your platform's requirements to see the minimums and plan to exceed that level when leading your sessions. Participants need to follow minimum guidelines to ensure success in attending, but for meeting leaders, presenters, trainers, and producers, it is a best practice to have more than the minimum recommendations. I personally have invested in the upgraded business plans for my home office internet connection, ensuring both my upload and download speeds are the highest available from my provider. When I am traveling and delivering sessions from a hotel, I will also always upgrade to the highest internet connection speed they offer.

It is also wise to have a backup in place for such things as internet outages, power loss, and teleconference failures. Internet connections come in different forms (such as ethernet, WiFi, and mobile phone hotspot) and easily switching to an alternative is a good practice if running live online sessions. It's something you will do on a regular basis.

Audio

Notice in the pictures of the offices that there is a hard-wired telephone, a backup mobile phone, and headsets for use with computer audio. Having more than one phone and even more than one headset available is a good practice. Switching to an alternative audio connection is only necessary if something is not working. Having backups in place is the best way to ensure you have options and do not have to end the session early if something stops working. I use various headsets for each, keeping them up to date as the technology changes. High quality sound as well as comfort are important to me given how much I am presenting and producing live online sessions. I rarely present using a cell phone; it's just a backup in case my computer audio or hardwired phone connection are not working.

As previously mentioned, audio is an area that is ever changing and continuously getting easier to manage. It is wise to stay up to date on technology changes in this area, as they are rapid and continuous. Of additional note is that computer audio quality is also connected to the speed of the internet connection. While I increasingly use computer audio to deliver and support my live online sessions, it remains very important to have the highest speed internet connections available.

Other Items

It's also a good idea to have everything nearby that you may need during a session and to make your physical space comfortable while you are live online. Things like paper and a pen come in handy when making notes on the technology, the participants, and anything else that might be happening during the session. Have some snacks (quiet ones!) within reach, and always have water or your beverage of choice available for refreshing your body and your voice. And be sure to include anything else to personalize your space and make it yours as all of this supports you to be the best and most authentic version of yourself as a presenter. I enjoy the view from my office windows, fresh flowers in a vase, and some of my favorite collectibles within my direct line of sight. (I am a vintage Barbie doll collector!) Each of these items brings me joy and helps set the tone in my voice for engaging participants.

Technology Checklist

There are quite a few technology feature details to take care of prior to the date of your live online session. It is easy to miss something or to be overwhelmed by all the options. I developed this list to help me and my team remember all the things that are necessary to consider when getting ready for a live online session. It has been extraordinarily helpful for those who are new to producing live online sessions and helps ensure they do not miss anything or find themselves surprised when something goes awry. Use this checklist as a guideline to your platform and all the technical details.

- ❏ **Login:** What is your login to the platform? Having the proper login will ensure you have all the platform capabilities available to manage and run your live online meeting, webinar, or virtual classroom session. If you use an attendee login, you will not be able to start the session. If you have a panelist login, you will not be able to start the session for the attendees. Check your login and confirm it is the proper one for the tasks required.

- ❏ **Location:** Will you be accessing the online meeting platform from a designated website, your email program, or through a learning management system? It is important to understand the different ways you can access the live online meeting technology that will host your session. A login to zoom.us to schedule and start a meeting is different than a login to a learning management system such as Litmos or Cornerstone. Additionally, creating a session from your email program will also look and act differently and may have limited feature options.

- ❏ **Platform Type:** Is your platform a Revealer or a Builder? (Refer to chapter 3 for descriptions of the types.) It's important to know whether materials will be uploaded in advance or shared in the moment the session is live. The plan forward for your content, presenters, and attendees is based on whether the platform is a Revealer or a Builder.

- ❏ **Set the Topic, Date, Time, and Duration:** Establish the session title and check the spelling. Select the date, time, time zone, and session duration. Confirm all details are correct and check the time zone again. Confirm the attendees will receive the correct information for their location, language, and time zone.

❑ **Organize or Upload Materials:** If your platform is a Revealer type, prepare a folder with all files that will be shared during the event. If the event has more than one session, create a separate folder for each session. Include all files that will be shared so there is no need to search or try to remember where each one is located once in front of an audience. Start the session and practice sharing everything. Join a second computer as an attendee to see how it all displays. If working in a Builder-type platform, open the room and upload the agenda or all the presentation and activity files that will be used for the event. Make sure they display as intended. Click through each slide, test the polls, create layouts, and arrange the pods and screens as permitted in your platform. Prepare breakout rooms and upload content into each one of them. Check that everything has loaded as expected. Click through all of it to confirm everything is in order. Start a session and join a second computer as an attendee to see how it all displays.

❑ **Set Up the Audio and Test It:** When scheduling or creating the session, choose or connect the audio, such as the teleconference or computer audio. Confirm the teleconference numbers are active and connected to your account and in working order. Open the session or a test session with the exact same settings and confirm it is working. Join a second computer as an attendee and walk through connecting the audio from the second computer's perspective. This is not the time for surprises! Know exactly how it will work and test it from both the leader and attendee angles.

❑ **Backup Platform:** Is it possible to have a backup platform in place? Sometimes platforms freeze or sites go down. If the Adobe Connect server is not responding, could you launch a Zoom meeting to conduct the session instead? If the platform is no longer working and disconnects everyone, could you switch to a teleconference? Quickly refer to your roster and email everyone the new teleconference numbers to call into and let the presenter explain the situation once everyone reconnects. This may not be realistic in all cases, but it is something to consider as a worst-case scenario to avoid canceling or ending a session early.

❑ **Backup Audio:** Should the teleconference go down, could you start a new one? Share a whiteboard with the new numbers and reconnect your audience. If computer audio stops working, could you start a teleconference and have the attendees call into that instead? These are options to be considered; though it is rare, sometimes plans do not work as outlined and having an alternative is a way to avoid canceling your live online session.

❑ **Identify Technical Support:** Determine how technical support will be provided to attendees once the live online session has begun. It is not realistic for a producer to provide one-on-one phone or email support at the same time they are also live online in the session. Decide who will accept calls and respond to emails if that is how attendees trying to enter session will be supported. If not, where will attendees who need help downloading or accessing the platform go for help?

Content Checklist

It is a common mistake to focus all production effort on the technical setup for a live online session, assuming all that is needed for the content is a set of slides. However, given all the features available to presenters, meeting hosts, and trainers, it is highly likely there is more content to take care of and manage than just one PowerPoint file. Below is a list of all the possibilities.

❑ **Slides and Presentation Materials:** Obtain the presentation materials, in the format and size that is compatible with your platform. Share or upload the materials in the environment to confirm they display as intended. PowerPoint slides are common, but they are not the only format presenters use. Obtain all other materials planned for the presentation such as PDF files, reports, or spreadsheets, depending on the intention of your live online session.

❑ **Handouts:** Obtain a copy of any handouts that will be provided to participants. Make them available for download, email them, or upload them into a file transfer location in the platform. Have a copy ready to send to participants in case they need it once the session begins.

❑ **Polls:** Prepare all polls in advance and connect or upload them to the session. Some platforms allow you to create separate polling files which are then launched when it's time, like Webex. Other platforms require polls be created from your profile and then attached to the session, like Zoom. And yet others, like Adobe Connect, allow the polls to be created in the room. Many platforms allow polls to be created on the site and placed in a shared content folder for use by all session hosts.

❑ **Breakouts:** If the session plans to use breakouts that have files associated with the activity, obtain the files the participants will need to reference. Upload them if your Builder-type platform allows it or have them ready to access in a folder if you are using a Revealer-type platform. Plan for how participants will receive the files, such as via email, file transfer, or pages in their handouts. Also plan for the number of breakouts needed, with the number of people to be assigned to each one. And check to see if the participants need to be assigned to a specific group, or if they can be randomly placed together.

❑ **Videos and Multimedia:** If there are any video, audio, or other multimedia files that need to be played during the live session, obtain these and have them ready for viewing. Test the files in advance by using your second computer logged in as an attendee. It's a leading practice to mute all attendee audio connections when playing multimedia to avoid feedback or interference. As a backup, consider making the multimedia files available in other ways in case they do not play as intended. For example, place the file on a shared site for download or make it available from a link sent to participants during the session.

❑ **Other Activities:** Obtain files, items, content, or instructions for any other types of activities that will run during the live session. Perhaps there will be items shown via a webcam like the hardware being demonstrated, or other physical items that may be part of a presentation such as a deck of cards.

Presenters Checklist

I'll always remember producing one of my first large webinars with a global client who had invited four presenters to speak and more than 1,000 attendees to join. We conducted a technical rehearsal with all the presenters a week in advance and everything was set up perfectly and ready to go.

On the day of the session, all but one of the presenters was online and ready to go. The fourth presenter could not connect. The reason? They were on a different computer, in a new location, with a different internet connection. Everything was different from what we had tested.

They did not realize when we did the technical rehearsal that those details mattered. So, the fourth presenter did not present that day, and I learned the lesson of being specific and thorough during testing.

I share this story as an example of why it's essential for the presenting and producing sides to be neatly aligned when getting ready for a virtual session. Use this checklist to avoid a similar mishap.

- ❏ **Contact:** If you are working with presenters other than yourself, obtain the following contact information: email, telephone number, and number for texting or instant messaging. All other contact information would be for purposes other than what is needed on the day of the live session, such as information for payments and other record keeping.

- ❏ **Invitation and Calendar Placeholder:** Send the presenters an invitation to the session. This might be a presenter-only link or a regular one, depending on your platform. Include a calendar placeholder, technical instructions, and a reminder to join the session early. A leading practice is to have presenters join at least 30 minutes early on the day of the live session.

- ❏ **Technical Rehearsal:** Schedule and conduct a session where every aspect of the technology will be tested. Use the same computer, internet connection, and audio connection that will be used on the day of the live session. Walk through each part of the platform the presenter intends to use, such as audio with headset, webcam, screen share, share presentation, polls, chat, feedback, whiteboards, and breakouts. Ensure each aspect of the technology is working properly by sharing, using, and launching each part of it. Be ready to teach presenters how to use the features of the platform but pay attention to time and set expectations accordingly.

❑ **Content Rehearsal:** Plan a content rehearsal with the presenters to give them a chance to practice what will be said, when it will be said, and how each segment will transition to the next. This will help with timing, getting comfortable on webcam, transitioning to other presenters, and paying attention to how long it takes to manage the technology while they are speaking. This rehearsal may be combined with the technical one but is usually best done separately as presenters tend to focus more on their speaking points than the technology, and time runs out. It is important to make clear that there is no presentation without the technology, and forgoing a technical rehearsal is risky.

❑ **In-Session Communication:** During the rehearsals and as part of the overall planning, decide how you will communicate with the presenters once the session is live with an audience. Instant messaging, private chat, or texting all work. People have their preferences, and whatever it is, confirm everyone agrees and will pay attention to it during the session. Refer to chapter 9 for more details on in-session communications with presenters and other producers as well as step-by-step rehearsal processes.

Attendees Checklist

The attendees are the most important part of your live online session, so it is certainly worth the time to ensure they have everything they need to be successful. Use this list to make sure you have sent all the required information to the attendees, and that they have everything in place to properly connect their computers and devices to the session on the correct date and time, with the materials they need to participate.

❑ **Roster:** Obtain a copy of the roster or the list of registrants. This is less for reporting, and more for quickly sending communications to participants should they need a handout, some extra information or help, or if a mass email is necessary due to a change in plans. Have the list open and minimized for quick reference during the live session.

❏ **Invitation:** Send communications, typically via email, to participants on the session details including content, timing, duration, and how to sign up if registration is required.

❏ **Welcome Email:** Once participants are confirmed for a session, send an email communication on how to join and participate in the live online session. Include not only the technical details for their computers and audio connections and materials, but also how to best set up their environment to actively participate in the live online session.

❏ **Calendar Placeholder:** Attendees do best when they have calendar placeholders containing the link, audio information, technical details, and materials all in one place. An email works well but it is easy to lose among all the other messages in one's inbox. A calendar placeholder places the information in a convenient view, and it's even better if it is set to have a reminder as well.

❏ **Technical Check:** Provide attendees with a way to perform a technical test for the system or device they intend to use to join the session. Most platforms have a link to join a test meeting or to do a premeeting diagnostic test, which will check a person's connection as well as their device. Type the name of your platform followed by the word "test" into an internet search to locate the link to send to all attendees ahead of time. If there is no link to do this, or you want to be more in control of the test, schedule and run a session for all your attendees to join at least a week before the live session is scheduled. (Please see chapter 8 for more details and examples of such a test session.)

❏ **Materials and Prework:** Confirm all materials and pre-assignments have been sent to attendees. Have a copy of them available for yourself and make sure all links are accessible and attachments have been received. It is a leading practice to have attendees download materials in advance if they need to use them during the session. Many presenters send materials following a session if they are going to be used as a follow-up resource or reference.

❏ **Reminder Email:** Send a reminder email to attendees containing the link, date, time, duration, content, technical information, and

any other important information they need to successfully participate in the live online session. Varying opinions exist regarding
the best number and cadence of reminder emails. At a minimum,
sending one the day before and one the hour before is an effective
strategy for providing information in the moment of need.

Going Live

After much learning, practicing, and preparing, everything is in order and
the time has come to log in, press the start button, begin the session, and
go live with an audience. The participants likely have high expectations.
The presenters are bound to be nervous, and if you are leading the production of the session, it is time to take a deep breath and put all your hard
work to the test. Let's review a step-by-step guide of what to expect and
the tasks to perform. It ends with a process of how to manage any problem
in the moment.

After setting up your own environment for the most effective and comfortable delivery of live online sessions, arrive in your space with water, coffee or
tea, and whatever else you need available during the session. Take a deep
breath, have one more sip of water, and start your session. The following steps
are in a general chronological order, but the specifics will change depending
on the details of your session. Use these as guideposts, editing as needed.

1. **Start early.** Open the session early so you have time to get
   everything in place and do a last-minute. Early may mean one
   hour, 30 minutes, 15 minutes, or five minutes. The amount of time
   depends on your level of experience, the needs of the presenters, and
   your personal preferences. A general rule is the larger the audience
   or the higher the stakes (for example, if executives are watching),
   then the more time you want to give yourself before attendees
   begin to arrive. For a regular online team meeting, five minutes is
   likely enough if you have prepared your agenda in advance. Open
   early enough to give yourself the time you need to best support the
   incoming audience and to ensure an on-time start.

2. **Open your own email.** If you are also providing support via
   your own email, have it open and be ready for emails to come in
   requesting help. You may not be able to manage the live session and

the emails at the same time, so it is a good practice to assign email support to another person or team of people, if possible.

3. **Join with second computer as an attendee.** As mentioned earlier, locate another computer to join as an attendee so you can view exactly how it looks for those attending your sessions. This will help you provide the most accurate support.

4. **Check the room settings.** Confirm all pods, panels, and layouts are enabled or in place. Check that session settings are enabled or disabled for things like attendee privileges, greeting messages, and waiting rooms.

5. **Confirm presentation is working and or loaded.** Check all presentation materials are loaded or will share properly.

6. **Check polls.** Load the polls in your Revealer-type platform or check to see that they are there and in working order in your Builder-type platform.

7. **Check all other content.** Confirm all files, multimedia, and websites that need to be shared are in place and ready to go.

8. **Check breakouts.** Check that the breakout rooms are set and have content loaded into them in your Builder-type platform, or confirm files are ready to be loaded when it is time in your Revealer-type platform.

9. **Open the participant registration list or roster and minimize.** Have the list of participants and their email addresses nearby and easily accessible. This can be used for tracking, contacting, and keeping notes about specific participants as needed throughout the session.

10. **Access the presentation notes, trainer manual, or facilitator guide.** A printed copy is an effective way to access the notes, the plan, or the manual for the session you are delivering or supporting. It is refreshing to look away from a computer screen to a printed copy of the plan, though obviously not required if it is not your preference. What matters is having your plan and notes in view and easily accessible.

11. **Open participant materials and minimize.** In addition to the presentation plan, also have a copy of the participants materials

either printed or at least open on your computer and minimized. This will help you support attendee questions throughout.

12. **Set the instant messaging program to ready.** Get situated on the instant messaging (or texting) program you will be using with your presenter and, if possible, other producers or people who you could call on in the session if you need additional assistance. (See chapter 9 on the advantages to having a team of people available on an instant messaging program.)

13. **Get presenters connected.** After opening the session, and confirming all materials are in place and ready to go, get your presenters connected. Call or email them if they are not in the session, and once they have connected, help them get comfortable.

14. **Test audio and webcams.** Once presenters have connected, test their audio connections. Make volume adjustments and practice muting and unmuting. Test their webcams and confirm they look as intended. Ask presenters to prepare in the waiting room, if you're using this feature, reviewing last-minute notes and getting ready to present. If it is a meeting or a virtual training session, help presenters greet people and start conversations if planned.

15. **Get attendees connected to the session.** This is the most important part of the long list of production tasks that you have focused on up until this point. Allow the attendees to begin joining the live session and begin supporting their needs. They may need help downloading the application, which is their responsibility to do from their own computers. They may need to contact technical support at your company, or perhaps with the platform company if they are unable to accept the commands needed for the technology to work properly on their computers. Web-based versions of the software are usually available as needed.

16. **Get attendees connected to the audio.** Audio will be the toughest part to support and will be where you spend most of your time. If a webinar is broadcasting audio and not requiring participants to speak, it will be easier. They just need to adjust their speakers and maintain their internet connections. When participants need to access a teleconference, or to connect their computer audio, you'll

need to be on alert to send messages via chat and help them as needed. They will likely not read the emails that have been sent and will ask for help via the chat the moment they connect.

17. **Greet people and provide support.** Be ready to provide connection information both verbally and via the chat for the 15 minutes leading up to the start time, and likely the first 15 minutes after the session has started. People will arrive early and late and will keep asking for help on how to connect and for access to any materials.

18. **Use a document with preplanned chat messages from which you can copy and paste.** Refer to your prepared chat messages document to quickly copy and paste common messages of support into the chat.

19. **Start the recording.** Begin recording the session just before the start time.

20. **Start on time.** Officially begin the session at the scheduled start time. Start according to the plans made with your presenters. Some producers begin the session by formally introducing the speakers, as is often the case with webinars. Other producers privately message presenters to let them know it is time to start. Work this process out during the rehearsal.

21. **Support the session throughout.** Once the session has begun, assist with all activities and plans as outlined. Follow along with presenters, listening in as they speak and helping them manage their presentation, the chat, the polls, the breakouts, and any other plans. Also listen and watch for attendees as they participate.

22. **Monitor audio.** Listen in on the audio to confirm it is technically working for everyone. Mute and unmute, help people connect and reconnect, and pay close attention to any changes or needs. Be ready to quickly mute all if needed. A quiet line will help everyone focus and allow you to zero in on any other problems.

23. **Monitor chat.** Watch for questions in the chat. Help the presenters monitor comments, ideas, and concerns. Many presenters will need help watching the chat at the same time they are presenting. Use the raise hand feedback icon or other process to interject, as worked out in your rehearsal.

24. **Monitor your instant messaging program.** Watch your instant messages in case presenters reach out for help this way. Use it to contact any other producers or support people if you need help.

25. **Take notes.** Take notes on anything that goes wrong for reference and follow up later. This should include what is happening with the technology, the presenters, the attendees, or the content that will need addressing or editing later.

26. **Prepare breakouts.** Try to have all attendees assigned to their breakouts about 10 minutes before the scheduled time of the small group activities. Be ahead of the process to allow time for changes and support if necessary.

27. **Stay alert.** Try to preempt problems by paying close attention to what is happening compared to what was planned. Listen to the presenters and attendees and respond quickly to provide them with the help they need.

28. **Take a break.** Be ready to run a break if the program has one in the schedule. You can share a countdown timer on your screen such as the one located at EggTimer.com. Stop sharing the timer and get the presenters back on track once the break has ended. Pass the presenter role back to them if needed. Help attendees get situated and ready to return.

29. **End the event.** Once the session has come to an end, be sure to stop the recording, save all files, and be the last person to exit the session. Refer to the follow-up checklist for additional tasks when closing the session.

Mixed Online and In-Person Audiences

Sometimes trainers, presenters, meeting leaders, and attendees are connected through online meeting technology instead of being present in-person. And other times, you may be online delivering a session where some attendees are also online, but many have gathered in one conference room, like my story in the opening of this chapter. Examples of mixed audiences:

- **Remote attendees:** When there are some attendees joining remotely using the virtual platform while the trainer, presenter, or meeting leader is on-site.

- **Remote presenter:** When the presenter is speaking from a remote location and typically on a screen that is projected to the attendees who are on-site.

It is challenging to engage an online audience when there is an on-site audience sitting right there, engaging in traditional nonverbal ways. Speakers are used to seeing actual raised hands, making in-person eye contact, and walking around a physical space to gauge an audience's interest and engagement. When an online audience is added to this arrangement, it is all too easy to forget they are even there because they cannot be seen, and often not even heard. Given this setup, it is even more important to consider the production of such sessions. It is my experience that the following practices are critical to ensure the online audience is also engaged.

Audio

Connect the trainer, presenter, or meeting leader to a high-quality audio connection. It is imperative the speaker can be heard or else those attending online do not need to be there at all. Additionally, those leading the sessions will need to hear from those attending online, so ensure online participants have a way to speak and be heard when they have questions, comments, and reports to share with the group. If the trainer, presenter, or meeting leader is remote, make sure they can be heard clearly by all the attendees on-site, and also make sure the speaker can hear the attendees as well. It is quite challenging to have no feedback from an audience; it is almost impossible to engage the audience if they cannot see or hear them.

Video

Optionally, also connect speakers and attendees to a camera for webcam viewing. If the technology is available, including the connection, it can be quite helpful for both the speaker and the attendees to be able to see one another.

Producer

Designate a person to manage the online audience and to act as the "go-between" for the speaker, the on-site attendees, and those joining remotely. This person not only manages the virtual meeting technology, but also conveys reactions, messages, and questions from the speaker to the audience and vice versa. Avoid making the mistake of thinking that the leader of the session can manage this as well as the on-site audience. Nonverbal communication is powerful, and it dominates a session—before the person leading it even realizes it, an hour will have gone by without a single check in with the online audience having ever occurred. This same person can also assist if it is the speaker who is remote, connecting questions and reactions to the remote speaker at planned intervals.

Activities

Plan for the on-site audience activities to occur as normal and make a specific plan for how those same activities will be executed to the online audience. For example, if on-site people turn to a neighbor to discuss something, assign remote participants to privately chat with another person online. Use breakout rooms for the online audience for longer activities where teams work on assignments, and be sure to call on a designated spokesperson who is properly connected to audio to share the online group's results. Ask the designated producer to share chat comments from the online audience to ensure they are included throughout the entire session.

Ending a Session and Following Up

I've always found it odd when a webinar window just closes as soon as the presenter says, "Thank you for coming." I prefer to close the window myself rather than looking at a message that says, "The host has ended this session. Goodbye." A thoughtful and professionally run session will pay attention to the ending process by ensuring everyone is ready to leave. This is also important for capturing any follow-up chat messages or questions that may not have been addressed during the live time together. I've had too many producers close a session on me before I have had the chance to take a few screenshots of my own or save some special private chat messages. Also, some of my best conversations have happened with attendees who stayed late hoping to ask an extra question or otherwise catch a few extra minutes with me. Wait until the attendees have exited the session and take the time to properly wrap up and close down a session to avoid these mistakes. Here are a few tips:

- ❑ **Stop and Save Recording:** Before closing the session, locate the recording controls and formally stop and save the recording. This ensures it is on its way to be processed.

- ❑ **Save Interactions:** Save chat messages, Q&A transcripts, polling results, annotated documents, breakout room activities, and anything else that was worked on during the live session as needed. Save these files to the designated content folder with an indication of the date for easy reference and follow-up later.

- ❑ **Final Remarks:** Before formally ending or closing the session, ensure all participants who are still logged in have been responded to or taken care of. Sometimes people stay on with additional questions or inquiries.

- ❑ **Close Event:** Press the close or end meeting option from the designated location in the menu bar. This will often prompt a reminder to save shared files and the recording as a reminder in case you have not already done so.

- ❑ **Gather Notes:** Take time to gather the notes you jotted down during the live session and reflect on them once the session has ended. This would include notes on anything unusual with the technology; any discrepancies, typos, or problems with content; feedback for the presenter; and issues with the attendees. Use these notes for your follow-up reports.

- ❑ **Report Technical Problems:** If technical problems occurred with your platform, it is important to document, and, if possible, take screen shots, of everything that went wrong. The more detail, the better the chance of a resolution. The technical support team will ask for this information when you report the errors. This helps them make improvements to the technology as well as properly support your account needs.

- ❑ **Obtain Recording:** Once the recording is available, listen to it to confirm it is in working order and make any edits as necessary. Determine how the recording will be shared—for example, downloaded or shared via a link—and note the process and information that will need to be shared with attendees.

❑ **Follow-Up Emails:** Send follow-up emails as planned: thank you emails to webinar attendees, what's next to virtual classroom participants, and agenda items to meeting attendees. Send reports to decisions makers, managers, supervisors, and other leaders who need to know about results from the session. Follow up on any technical problems as needed. Be sure to include assignments, next steps, resources, recording access, and other pertinent information related to the session.

Conclusion

Producing a live online session is quite the undertaking, but by focusing on the skills needed to be successful, understanding the different types of platforms and their features, and properly preparing for every detail along the way, effectively managing a live delivery is an exhilarating experience! In the next chapter, we'll take a look at all the things that could go wrong despite all the plans you have put in place. Sometimes things just do not work, and having insight into what those might be will help you build the confidence needed to continue enjoying producing live online sessions for years to come.

Reflection Questions

▶ What is one change you intend to make to better set up your workspace for virtual session delivery?

▶ There are quite a few details on each checklist for the technology, the content, the presenters, and the attendees. Which ones are new to you? Which ones require your immediate attention?

▶ What steps in going live concern you the most? That section in the chapter is key. I suggest printing that list! Download "Producing a Virtual Session" from my website, KassyConsulting.com.

Troubleshooting the Virtual Platform

In This Chapter

- A three-step process to manage when things go wrong in front of a live audience
- Common problems with virtual platform features and solutions for each
- A quick reference checklist: Troubleshooting Questions to Solve Common Virtual Session Problems

Even the best-laid plans do not always go as expected, so being prepared to respond quickly, in front of an audience, is a crucial part of producing a live online session. I once lost power while delivering a virtual training, which of course kicked me off the session. Fortunately I was working with a producer who could easily take over and continue while I quickly joined the audio from my cell phone. I asked my producer to move the slides and manage the online platform without me. I referred to my printed trainer manual and kept going. But it got worse—the storm that made me lose power must have been traveling through the country that day because moments later my producer also lost power! At that point, one of the attendees was automatically given the role of host to control the session. (We were in Webex, and that's how that platform works—automatically transferring control to the next person in the participant list.) So I just taught the class from my phone while that attendee controlled it for all the others at my verbal guidance. This was certainly not an ideal situation, but it was incredible to be able to continue the training session without having to cancel. Knowing the details of the web conferencing platform I was working with, as well as all the features and how they function, was what enabled me to survive the problems.

The story just described was extreme. Most technical problems with your live online platform are not like what I experienced, and in fact, many are not even technical problems at all. Always begin addressing a technical issue by confirming that the features are in fact included with your platform, that they are enabled and connected to the session, and that session leaders and participants know how to use the features before assuming something is broken. So many "technical issues" can be resolved by simply showing people where the features are located, and the exact steps they need to follow to make them work.

For example, it is often assumed that polling is not working, when in fact the poll was simply not created ahead of time and connected to the session. Some platforms require polls to be made in advance and then attached to the session before it begins.

When Things Go Wrong in Front of a Live Online Audience: The RPA Process

Once you've confirmed it's not a simple matter of the feature not being enabled and something is in fact going wrong, use the RPA (relax, pinpoint, act) process to help identify what is happening and how best to move forward with a solution (Figure 6-1). To start, here is the overall process to follow during a live session when something is not working. The P in this process requires you to pinpoint the problem and, in this chapter, we examine all that could be happening with each feature.

Relax: Attendees are listening in and watching every move being made by those leading the online session. They follow the cues of those presenting and producing, so it is your responsibility to keep them calm and paying attention to what they should do next. It is important to take a deep breath and proceed with your examination of the problem. Mute your line if needed and take a drink of water. This first step will help you focus and be clearer as you determine what is wrong.

Pinpoint: Unmute your line and let the attendees know something is happening, and begin to examine the likely cause of the problem. Identify the source of the problem first: Is it the presenter, one attendee, or all attendees? Is it the platform, the audio, or the content? Problem solving for one person is different than for the entire audience, so identify the exact problem as quickly as possible to determine the next steps.

Act: Recall the acronym we introduced in chapter 3—ACT: access, click, team up. The solution lies in your knowledge of the platform features and your preparation of the plan for that session. If a poll is not launching, then ask the presenter to use the slide for the question and the chat for the answers. If breakouts won't launch, pair people up in teams of two to privately chat instead, or just make it a full group activity. If slides are no longer showing, take the presenter controls back and reload the slides. If audio goes down, reconnect people, restart it, or switch to the back up. Each of these example solutions exists as a result of knowing what the platform is supposed to do and being aware of what other capabilities are available should the need arise.

The answer to resolving problems in front of a live audience lies in your level of knowledge of the platform and all your advance preparation. You've got this!

Figure 6-1. The RPA Process

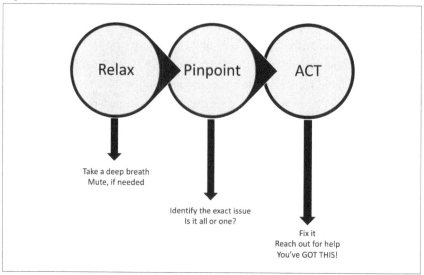

Let's revisit the list of common in-session features, this time reviewing what might go wrong with each so you can quickly identify what to do to get things back on track.

Get Started Features

As in chapter 4 on the learning the features, the "get started" features include roles, audio, participant list, webcam, and recording.

Roles

The most common problem related to roles is not realizing they exist or that there are important differences between them. I can't even count how many times I have heard this: "What do you mean there is a host and a presenter? What's a host? Isn't it all the same thing?" Many technical issues are due to not being in the role needed to perform the task at hand. Problems using the platform happen when someone is not assigned the role they need in order to access or control what is being requested of them, such as start a session, share slides, or launch a poll. So, the first line of technical support for this feature is knowledge: What roles does your platform have and what features can each role control? Host, organizer, co-host, presenter, panelist, participant, and attendee are a few of the most common options.

Roles get confusing across all the different platforms. In GoToMeeting, it is the organizer who has the most control, whereas in Webex it is the host even though the presenter is the one who shares their screen. In Zoom everyone can take turns sharing, but only the host and co-hosts could launch polling and only the host can manage the breakouts. It is also the case that settings can be adjusted to change the role permissions from the defaults. It's easy to get confused and important to know exactly what roles your platform has and how it labels each, so you are not caught off guard and unable to do what you've planned.

Here are three specific problems that involve roles: starting a session, launching a poll or moving a slide, and needing to pass presenter controls to another person.

You can't start the session. A session cannot be started without logging into the site as a host or organizer. Similarly, a session cannot be joined by a participant using the host link as that link will ask them to login as the host and start, rather than join, the session. Make sure the link or invite sent to participants is for them to register or join and that you have not accidentally forwarded your host link to them.

You can't launch a poll or move a slide. A common mistake occurs when a host and a presenter are running a session together, the presenter is ready for the poll and wants the host to launch it. The host tries to do it but the feature is inactive for them. Sometimes, the presenter role is needed in order to launch polls. In this moment, it is necessary for the host to take the presenter role and then the poll will be active for them to launch. They then need to pass the presenter role back to the speaker so they can proceed with moving their own slides, sharing content, and so on.

You need to make someone else the presenter. The role that has the login to the site (such as the host or organizer) and creates and starts a session is usually the one who can designate all the other roles. Hosts promote attendees to presenter, act as co-host, and usually can take the designation away as well. When scheduling a session, there is typically a special presenter invitation that will provide those designated to present with a special link, thus promoting them to presenter as soon as they join the session using that link.

Understanding the differences between the roles, specifically in terms of the features and capabilities available to each one, is the first step in taking care of technical problems.

Audio

Audio is one of the most common areas for technical issues in live online sessions, so an important production task is to be well versed in the audio requirements of the platform. Confusion about audio requirements, connectivity problems, integration issues, and improper equipment are just a few of the reasons why webinars, live virtual trainings, and online meetings have trouble starting on time and then suffer other problems throughout. Additional confusion exists surrounding the differences between teleconferences, where attendees call in versus receive a call back, and whether those telephone lines are integrated with the platform or not. Also confusing is how to properly connect using computer audio, otherwise known as VoIP. And lastly, talking while muted is one of the most common, and sometimes funny, technical problems you will face on a regular basis in your live online sessions. Make sure you and your participants know how to manage the mute feature. Someday I plan to run a "What Not to Do" webinar on just audio problems alone. One of my personal favorites was when we got taken to the restroom in an online meeting with a group of executives and the CFO made a joke that "Someone must be joining from Flushing, New York!"

Let's start with specific teleconference problems before moving to computer audio.

Teleconference Problems

Participants are just calling in. Many attendees do not know how to properly connect to an online meeting, so they usually default to just calling in. Many session organizers send the phone numbers in the email invitation, which unintentionally encourages attendees to never learn how to properly locate and connect to the session's audio. Consider sending instructions on how to properly connect, rather than the phone numbers, to avoid having people just calling in. Even if they're joining using a mobile device, it is still necessary to download the mobile application of the platform. Also remember that while a mobile device may be a convenient way to join an online meeting or listen in on a webinar, it is likely not acceptable for presenters to lead a session from or for participants to fully participate in collaborative learning sessions.

Where are these phone numbers coming from? When using a teleconference, it is necessary to know if the numbers are provided by the online meeting platform itself or if they are being supplied by a separate or third-party web teleconferencing provider. Either way, make sure the teleconference is properly integrated with your platform or that the information on how to dial in separately is clear to everyone so that it works smoothly for the attendees. As a producer, be sure to know how to control the teleconference in the following areas, whether it is integrated or not: starting, ending, muting, unmuting, recording, and breakout room integration.

Whose number is that? Aligning phone numbers to attendees in the participant list is a frustrating and often difficult production task to manage in an online session. Many platforms have teleconferences integrated with the system, and in order for the teleconference connection to be visually connected to the participant's name in the attendee list, they need to accept the call back and confirm it by pressing a button on their phones, or dial in to the teleconference and reference their attendee or participant ID number. Most participants do not realize this is needed and the result is a person's name in the list and a separate listing for their phone number. Depending on the platform, this may say "call-in user" or may simply be a phone number added to the attendee list. The solution is for participants to follow the instructions—but when they don't, they'll likely need to hang up and dial back into the teleconference, following the prompts to enter their ID numbers. Some systems allow an attendee to enter the ID number afterward, and other systems like Adobe Connect and Zoom have a function where the hosts can select the name and the number and merge the two together. I love this feature, but things do get awkward if you merge the wrong phone number and person. I've done that more than once and the only way I know to fix it is to have everyone affected exit the session and reconnect. Oops!

When participants are or need to be muted. It is important to know how muting works and how to control it for the entire audience. For virtual classroom sessions and meetings, teach people how to manage their own mute button, both on their phones and using the platform interface. Hearing music, background noise, construction sounds, animals, and other people in the background are just a few of the many problems a lack of muting will bring to your session. Participants often enter sessions assuming they cannot be heard so they do not pay attention. Communicate with them and keep your focus on the audio right from the moment your session begins. Use "mute upon entry" when running a large online webinar, and be sure to always provide unmute warnings to participants prior to unmuting them. Find out whether a participant can unmute themselves if they have been muted by the host or leader of the session. Sometimes they won't be able to, and it will require the leader of the session to do it instead.

Computer Audio (VoIP) Problems

Where is the echo and feedback coming from? As of the writing of this book, computer audio is increasingly becoming the preferred method of audio in a live online session. The technology gets better each day, participants are more familiar with the process, and the cost is minimal or sometimes free. However, problems using computer audio can be the most irritating of all the audio issues; it is important to have the proper equipment and sound settings for it to work effectively. Echoes and feedback are the most common issue, often stopping a presenter from continuing to speak, let alone think, due to the level of disruption it causes for the entire session. Most echo and feedback issues occur when a participant has not properly connected a headset, air pods, microphone, or other audio device to their computer, and instead simply uses the built-in speakers and microphones on their computers. When a speaker uses a computer's built-in microphone and speakers (rather than headphones, earbuds, or a headset), the sound of their own voice simultaneously broadcasts from their own speakers, creating a feedback loop or echo that will intensify until they are muted.

Follow these steps to troubleshoot when computer audio connections have an echo or feedback:

1. Quickly mute the offending line or entire conference to silence the problem in the moment.
2. Communicate the proper way to connect to the audio via an announcement, a message in chat, or on a prepared slide.
3. Get the speaker back on track and use chat to keep connecting with those who need computer audio help.

4. If needed, contact participants who need help via a one-on-one phone call.

Who gets to speak and when? Enabling microphones is typically required of most platforms. Many systems that support computer audio will default to allowing participants to hear the speaker's audio as it is transmitted out to the audience but require attendees' microphones to be enabled for them to chime in. Another problem with computer audio may be that the participant needs to click on a button requesting permission to speak. Depending on the settings of your platform, participants may have to take turns, and asking to speak might be required before they can be heard.

When participants are or need to be muted. As with teleconference, computer audio also needs to be unmuted when a participant wishes to speak. Be sure they have unmuted themselves, or that you have done it for them, when they have requested permission to speak. I think we would all agree that never again hearing or saying the phrase "Can you hear me now?" would be a welcomed relief.

Participant List

Problems with the participant list itself are uncommon, but it is worthy of mention since this list often provides important information for other technical problems a participant may be experiencing. Problems concerning audio connectivity can usually be seen or indicated in the list of participants, because the icons indicate how a participant has joined a session and in some cases the strength of their connection as well. When producing a session, be sure you can view the participant list, even if it is not necessary for the other attendees to see it (as in large online webinars and webcasts). The participant list may need to be expanded if it is minimized or activated if it is hidden. Also, if attention tracking is needed, ensure that feature is included and enabled.

Webcam

The webcam isn't working. Getting the web conferencing platform to recognize your webcam is the most common problem people have with this feature. Sometimes a person will join a webinar and click the button to show the webcam and nothing happens. In this instance, ask the person to leave the session, close all the windows and applications they have open on their computer, and then rejoin the session. Sometimes a full restart of the computer is required, but the platform will typically initialize the webcam properly on a second try. In some cases, it may be necessary to access the camera settings on the computer rather than in the platform. The platform may not be able to access the webcam if the camera settings in your operating system are not permitting it, or if the webcam is associated with another application, such as Skype or Microsoft Teams, that is not the one being used for the web conference.

I don't know how to be on camera. This is an example of a time when it's not the case that the feature is not working, but rather the person using the feature is not using it correctly. Knowing exactly when you are on camera is a common issue and, in some cases, an embarrassing one. Make sure you know when you are appearing on camera, and be certain what people see is what you want them to see. Setting up your environment and looking good on webcam is important for establishing credibility and respect. Do not be caught off guard: Know exactly how the camera works and when you will appear on it. Many web conferencing platforms have settings where the camera can view everyone at once, or just the person speaking. In today's world where it is more common to be working remotely or from home offices, it is imperative to know when you are on camera and how you look to those who can see you. Avoid the embarrassment of awkward angles that reveal too much or forgetting to turn off the camera if you step away. People can see what you are doing, as well as what is around you. Show up on webcam in the same way you would show up to a meeting in a conference room or in an office. (Tips and techniques for looking great on webcam are outlined in chapter 4.)

Recording

I forgot to record the sound. The most common problem when making a recording of a live online meeting, training, or webinar is ensuring the audio was also recorded. Always make a test recording ahead of time to confirm the audio connection that will be used for the session is also included. Most platforms have the option to record, but make sure it is enabled for the session, and that the audio provider that is connected to the session will also be included in the final file. Do not assume, especially when a teleconference is provided by a separate vendor, that the recording in the platform will also capture the sound from the teleconference. Some platforms require the option to record be enabled at an administrative level. If the option is not there, check with your administrator to see if it is disabled or if recording is not permitted at all on your site.

Recording when you do not intend to. Don't make the same mistake that I once did and leave the recording on while your participants are in break-outs. A recording exists of me fixing my hair, having a snack, and singing along to one of my favorite songs while participants were hard at work on a role play. I had no idea until a participant who could not attend the class that day sent me a note saying they had really enjoyed that part of the class!

You don't have any recording options. Additionally, not all roles are permitted to record a session. Make sure you have joined the session as a host, presenter, organizer, or other lead role so you're able to press the start record button. Check for a pause button on the control panel and remember to begin recording again after pausing. Also be sure to end or stop the recording so that it is properly saved where indicated. Once the file is saved, look to see if it was saved locally to your computer or if it will be stored on the platform's site. Check your profile for a section with recordings and look for the file to download or the link to send for participants to access it.

The recording file won't play. Once a file is created, check that the file type is compatible with the systems your participants use. Many platforms will host the file for you, generating a link to share. This link can often be password protected and set to allow download or online viewing only. Most platforms also have recording access reporting capabilities as well. Again, this feature is typically located in the profile of the host or the site administrator.

You need to edit the recording. One final concern with recordings is the need to edit the recording once it has been created. Presentations often contain mistakes, and participants may do or say things that would be best edited out. Editing a recording will require it to first be downloaded from the platform's server and then shared or posted for participant viewing. Some platforms, like Webex, have editors for the recording files since the file type is proprietary to that platform. You can download the recording editor from the recording section of your profile or your platform's site. Other platforms like Zoom create recordings in standard file types like MP4 so you can use any editing program that is compatible with those file types. Be sure to share or post the recording in a place that's accessible to those who need to view or edit it.

One final support tip: view the recording before sharing it with anyone else. It may not have recorded properly, and it is better to know that before sending out mistaken information.

Basic Interaction Features

The basic interaction features include feedback, chat, whiteboard, annotation, share file, and share screen.

Feedback

Feedback icons are a simple feature that you can request participants use during an online session, such as "raise hand," "green check," and "away." This is my favorite feature. I like using it throughout the entire session, asking people to click the icons to let me know they are there, in the same way I look for nonverbal communication cues when I am in person. Don't overlook this simple tool, because if you have ever heard yourself saying, "Who has a question?" or "Who would like to share more about that?" and gotten no response, you simply forgot to tell them to raise their hand or click the thumbs up.

Participants don't know the feedback feature exists or how to use it. Assuming the feature is enabled, the most common issue with the feedback tools is that participants don't know where they are located or if they should use them. People do not usually click on things unless specifically requested, so often the feedback tools go unused. Sometimes attendees are using the feedback icons to raise their hand or to indicate the presenter should slow down and the presenter is completely unaware of them. Make sure if you are presenting, or if you are producing for a presenter, to review where the feedback icons are located, situate them where you can see them, and ask attendees for feedback throughout. Make a point to pay attention to this important and simple-to-use feature as it is one of the easiest ways to overcome the fear of presenting to an audience that is not paying attention!

You don't see any options for feedback. If there are no feedback tools in the platform you are using, it could be that they are not enabled, like in the case of Zoom, or it could be that there are not very many to use, like in the case of Webex Meeting Center, where the only feedback option is a button to raise one's hand. Check the platform settings to see if they need to be enabled or if they can be adjusted in advance.

Chat

Chat is the least likely feature to have issues as it is so frequently and easily used in online meetings, training, and webinars. People know how to use chat, but sometimes they don't use it correctly or they don't pay attention to it at all. The main issues with chat have more to do with behavior than technical function, but when technical problems occur it is usually due to attendee privileges or settings.

Chatversations are conversations between participants, trainers, presenters, and producers using the chat feature, and they are both engaging and effective. I am especially pleased when participants help one another using the chat and give comments on one another's message while we are live in a session. This is a true testament of the power of the community and social learning that virtual sessions can support.

You (or participants) can't send a chat to the person intended. Recall the discussion on roles from the previous chapter? Chat privileges often default to only allowing leaders of sessions to send public chat messages and allowing participants to only send messages to the leaders. This is for privacy concerns since many webinars are public, so this default setting controls what is seen. Check the attendee privileges to ensure the proper settings are selected.

Participants can't type a message. Sometimes participants will have trouble figuring out exactly where to type messages. It is helpful to have a screen shot during the opening of the session to show them exactly where to locate the chat area and where to type their messages.

Disruptive or distracting chat messages. Sometimes chat messages can get out of control and disruptive messages find their way to a public audience. This most often happens when presenters are boring or are not in control of the audience. Disruptive chat is more common in large audiences than it is in small group meetings and training sessions. It is helpful to watch the chat and to let people know how to use the chat, who can see their messages, and what is expected of them throughout the session. When participants know these details, they tend to follow instructions. It is when you leave it to them to figure out, or you don't pay attention, or you don't know what you are doing, that trouble may arise.

Strong production skills will prevent problems with chat, since setting the privileges in advance and knowing exactly how it operates in your specific platform will prevent issues from happening. But if something inappropriate is sent in a public chat, follow these three steps to quickly address the situation:

1. Clear the chat messages if the platform allows it, or if not, type a series of "+" signs into the chat, one at a time, until the disruptive message is out of view.
2. Disable the public chat.
3. Optionally make a verbal announcement to ask participants to use the chat appropriately and in alignment with session guidelines.

Whiteboard

Using a whiteboard in an online meeting is relatively common, assuming meeting attendees know they have it available to them. Whiteboard has two meanings: as a noun, it is a blank "board" that can be shared and then annotated upon. As a verb, it means to annotate or draw upon something. The first technical problem with the whiteboard is knowing it exists, and then showing people how to use the annotation tools that accompany it.

The presenter lost their place. Whiteboards exist separately from other files that have been uploaded or shared into the environment. Sometimes, presenters get lost finding their way back to their prepared files once they have shared a whiteboard to illustrate a process or to collaborate with team members. Look to the list of shared content to find where to click to take a presenter back to their prepared content. It could be minimized or in a drop down or simply on another tab, panel, pod, or layout, depending on the platform you are using.

You need to save the whiteboard work. Saving a whiteboard can also become an issue, both in the main meeting, as well as in breakout rooms. Remember to save the whiteboard in a format that is viewable outside the meeting. If there is no way to save it, then use a screen capturing tool to make your own copy as an image file. Take note of where you save the file and remember to share it with any interested parties as needed.

Many files, whether uploaded into a Builder environment, or shared in a Revealer environment, can be whiteboarded or annotated upon. Learning to use the annotation tools on a whiteboard remains as challenging as it was years ago when I first started! Screenshots and live screen shares help, but honestly, just guiding the attendees to use the annotation tools on an activity related to the topic is the best way. See the next section for technical issues surrounding the use of this time-saving technique as well as other problems with sharing the space using the annotation tools.

Annotation

If the annotation tools are not working, it is likely because they have not been enabled. If these tools exist in your platform, it is usually the case that only the host, organizers, and presenters can use them by default. They can be used on whiteboards and often on uploaded or shared files as well. If attendees need to use annotation tools, then be certain the privilege is enabled for them to do so. This is typically done in the meeting settings, and sometimes in the account settings.

Annotation tools are not working or are out of control. Once attendees can annotate, they will need training on how to use the various tools available. They will often struggle with locating the tools, clicking on and off them, and doing what is needed for their annotations to be seen. Most annotations are seen once a person clicks away, or if they press enter on their keyboard.

Visual chaos. To manage space on a whiteboard, be aware of how many people are typing on it at once. Control this by adding names to spaces, placing pointers, or only permitting limited numbers of people to type at any given time.

You want to save the annotations. Don't forget to save annotations if needed by looking for a save button on the annotation toolbar or from one of the menu options in the platform. In Revealer-type platforms annotations often need to be cleared before moving on, otherwise they remain on the screen.

Share File

Sharing a file is a feature in a builder's environment where certain types of files can be uploaded into the environment, whether that is the session window or a pod or other designated area.

You don't want to share your screen. The first line of technical support for this feature is knowing that it exists as an option, and that it is different from sharing one's screen to the application in which the file was created. Sharing a file in this way means uploading it so that once it is visible in the session environment, it is no longer being displayed in the application in which it was created.

The file won't upload or doesn't upload properly. For example, if you're sharing a PowerPoint file, it will no longer be running through the application of PowerPoint with the standard PowerPoint tools for presenting. Instead, it gets converted when it uploads, and since it needs to be converted, it is important to confirm the file is compatible with your platform. Check the "files of type" box. It is an additional box usually just under the "file name" box when searching for a file to upload. The fonts you have used may not translate and may be converted back to something like Arial or Times New Roman. Also, images and text boxes may not stay in place and may then overlap one another. You may need to save the slide as an image to keep it in place, rather than have multiple images or elements on the slide that get moved around during the upload and conversion process.

Another problem with sharing files could be size. Files that are hundreds of megabytes may be too large to upload into the environment, and it will time out or sometimes even shut down your meeting!

Share Screen

The most popular presenter's feature is screen sharing. As covered in the features chapter, sharing one's screen can include the sharing entire desktop, one application at a time, or only designated portions of the screen.

Oversharing. Sometimes presenters do not pay enough attention and simply click the first button available, not realizing just how much is being shared. This is the main technical problem with screen sharing: revealing too much or "oversharing." Ask the presenter to share the one application they want to show the audience rather than their entire desktop where their email or instant messaging application could also be revealed. Also, ask the presenter to close any other applications that may be open and running on their computer, including those that might have pop-up notifications enabled. This will not only protect them from sharing too much, but also improve the performance of their computer since less processing power will be in use.

Everyone saw that instant message. When sharing your screen, be sure to close, disable, or move your instant messaging program to another monitor. There have been way too many mistakenly shared instant messages in online meetings, and you want to avoid this at all costs.

Participants cannot see the shared content. Conversely, the second problem is revealing too little, or "under-sharing." Perhaps the presenter is sharing their screen, but the attendees see nothing, a blank screen, or even a window with crossed lines in it, otherwise known as a "waffle screen." This means the presenter shared an application but then has clicked to a different one. They need to share the correct application or choose to share their entire screen if more than one application will be necessary for participants to view.

There is no option to share screen. Another technical problem with screen sharing is not having the proper role or privilege, which results in the option for screen sharing appearing inactive. Select the person's name who needs to share and make sure they have the role or the privilege needed in order to share.

Screen sharing froze. Other technical problems occur when screen sharing freezes or stops working. In this case, just take the role of the presenter away from the person sharing. This will either unfreeze them or do nothing. If it does nothing, ask them to fully restart their computer and rejoin the session. Hand the presenter controls back to them once they rejoin.

Unintentional sharing. And finally, sometimes an attendee will share their screen without intending to take over the presentation or meeting! Webex Meeting Center and Zoom both have settings to allow all attendees to screen share. This is setup to make collaborative meetings faster and easier, but when someone does it unintentionally, it is disruptive and perhaps embarrassing. Disable the permission, privilege, or setting either in the account settings, or in the meeting settings themselves.

Advanced Interaction

The advanced interaction features include polling, notes, Q&A, file transfer, and breakout.

Polling

When polls have issues, it is usually because they have not been prepared in advance. Most platforms will allow session hosts to create and attach polls to sessions at an administrative level. Many systems even allow for those polls to be shared to a content library, allowing other hosts to use them as well. It doesn't make sense to write the questions and accompanying answers while an audience waits, so it is always a best practice to create them in advance and be sure they are ready to launch when the presenter requests it.

The results are not showing. Always remember to close the poll and then decide if broadcasting the results is needed. Sometimes polls have timers and will close automatically. Once a poll is closed, it does not always show the results and usually needs a separate check box to allow the results to be seen. Also check the format of the shared results: If a webinar has small attendance, it may be better to share the percentage of results rather than the actual numbers.

You lost the results. Also remember to save the results if you might need them later. Some platforms automatically save them like Adobe Connect and Zoom, while others require a formal save like in Webex, which will prompt you to save before passing the presenter role to someone else or before closing the session.

Be on the lookout for the overuse of polls. I have worked with many clients who are required to share "six polls for every hour of live online time to prove engagement." I really do not think this is "engaging" anyone other than perhaps the person launching the polls, so I encourage you to seek out alternatives if possible!

Notes

Technical issues with notes usually arise when privileges have not been properly set to use them or the feature itself has not been enabled. Be sure to determine who is taking notes—one person to share with everyone, or each person taking their own—and then confirm the session settings are in alignment with the plan.

No one can see the notes. Sometimes people cannot see the notes, so make sure if a designated note-taker has been identified, that they know how to broadcast or share their notes for the entire audience to view. Also be sure to save the notes so they can be properly distributed following the meeting, if requested.

Q&A

Having a designated space to manage questions is helpful in large audience events. It helps keep things organized, private, and in control. The main problem with a Q&A panel or pod is just knowing that it exists and then using it properly. Typically, the person managing the questions coming in needs to have a leader role within the session such as host, co-host, panelist, or organizer. Make sure the person or people tasked to manage questions are promoted to the role needed.

Responses are not visible, or you are unable to answer a question. Questions typically come in privately to the leaders of a session. They can click on each, respond, and decide to send an answer back publicly to the entire audience, or privately to the person who submitted the question. Sometimes when multiple leaders are responding to questions, they may find one they want to answer is not available for a response. This usually means that another leader is responding to it and they simply need to wait until that leader has answered, then they can also respond. Some systems do not allow this, so check your platform to be certain.

Participants don't know how to submit questions. Usually, participants need to be shown where and how to submit questions, and some programs like GoToWebinar only allow one question to be submitted at a time, meaning that the person's question needs to be answered before they can submit another one. Be careful of this in a training session as participants may have more than one question they need answered. If this is the case, it might be best to manage questions via the chat instead.

File Transfer

Offering files or handouts for participants to download is a convenient feature, especially when asking attendees to participate in activities that are too complex for the whiteboard and annotation features. However, they come with their own set of challenges.

The file will not load. When this feature doesn't work, it is usually because it has not been enabled, or the file size or type is not compatible with the system. Most of the time, online meeting platforms use a standard file transfer protocol (FTP) process for this feature, and usually there are no restrictions. But as is the case with any software program, check your platform's system requirements if you are experiencing issues while attempting to upload a file for participants to download.

Where is the file? Many platforms have a designated area for file transfer like Adobe Connect where a file transfer pod can be placed wherever you choose. Some platforms, like Zoom, use the chat, and yet others, like Webex, will launch a pop-up window when the file transfer is initiated. In the case of Zoom, be sure to enable the file transfer option in your profile's settings so that it is available in your sessions. Be sure to tell participants exactly where to download the file from as it often goes unnoticed. They will likely need instructions on exactly how to download it, and where it saves to their computers once it has been downloaded. Again, check with your platform to verify the exact steps on where to click to save, and where the files get placed once they are saved.

Breakout

Breakout rooms are both feared and loved at the same time. They are feared when hosts, presenters, and trainers do not know how to manage them, and they are loved once hosts, presenters, and trainers figure out how to manage them confidently.

You don't see the breakout option. The first problem with breakouts is when they don't exist. Not all live online platforms include this feature as part of the system. For example, only Webex Training Center has them, not Webex Meeting or Event Center. Likewise, only GoToTraining has breakouts, not GoToMeeting or GoToWebinar. Make sure your host or organizer login is to the platform that has the features you need.

It is typically the case that only a leader-level role will be able to create and manage the breakout rooms. Be sure to have the role necessary, and that you have it early enough to plan the breakouts, so no time is lost in the process. It may be that you can pre-assign participants to breakout rooms, but to do this, most platforms require each participant email address to be registered with the session ahead of time. Require registration on the session if this is a part of the breakout room functionality you intend to use. Otherwise, most producers assign participants to breakouts once the session has started, and once each person has joined.

Participants are not entering their breakout rooms. Be clear on how the breakout messaging works in your platform. Some platforms send pop-up messages requesting participants click to agree to lead and join breakouts. If they are not joining their breakout, they may not be clicking the agree button to begin the process.

I've learned the hard way that I need to have breakout leaders raise their hand to agree to lead their breakout group before sending them off. It's slightly embarrassing to launch the breakouts and have some people just do nothing because they were not even at their desks at the time! For Zoom and Adobe Connect, this won't matter as people can go into a breakout without a leader, but for Webex, the leader opens the room, so if the leader is not there, the team members just sit there waiting, unable to enter the room at all.

Participants cannot hear one another. Audio connections with break-outs are the most challenging thing to manage. It is imperative participants properly connect to the audio portion of your live online session if you intend to use the breakout rooms. If a participant has dialed in and their teleconference connection is not listed next to their name in the participants list, it likely means they did not enter in their attendee ID when they called in. The system does not know which teleconference connection belongs to that participant, so when they get placed into a breakout, their audio connection will not follow them. Check to see if you can manually send their teleconference connection to the breakout room, which of course assumes you know which one belongs to each person. Or, ask the participants who have not done this to hang up and call back in, referencing their attendee ID number.

No one can hear each other once the breakouts have ended. Occasionally, the audio will not switch back from the breakouts and no one can hear one another once the breakouts have ended. In this case, it is recommended to have everyone disconnect from the session completely and to come back in to start again. It's the classic "restart and rejoin" technical support option that will fix this in most cases.

You (or participants) have problems sharing the work. Some platforms like Adobe Connect will automatically save whiteboards participants have worked on in their breakouts, while others like Zoom will require participants save it themselves. If the work is not there as expected, asking participants to share their screens to display their work is a nice alternative, or simply ask them to describe it over audio rather than showing it. Another way to pre-empt this type of problem is to join each breakout ahead of time and take a screenshot of their work for them. You could also request participants email their work to the trainer and then the trainer can share their screen to show all the received files.

Leaders cannot visit the breakouts. The most likely problem here is they were not assigned the role necessary to move from breakout to breakout. Make sure they are a host, co-host, presenter, panelist, organizer, or other leadership role in your platform. The other issue may be that the leader has not clicked on the correct spot to activate the "join breakout" button. Be sure they have selected the proper option to join each breakout.

Conclusion

Even when things go wrong or something unexpected happens, controlling the production tasks can become a fondly remembered story like the many I have shared with you throughout this chapter. A job well done feels great, but one that was well done despite great obstacles feels even better! In the next chapter, we'll examine the instructional design techniques for including the production tasks as part of program materials and other development plans.

Reflection Questions

▸ Think about the worst virtual session problem you have experienced. How was it managed?

▸ Which part of the RPA process will you focus on learning to implement first?

▸ Of all the problems listed in this chapter, which one has you most concerned? What will you do to manage this concern? Use Table 6-1 for troubleshooting questions for common virtual session problems.

Table 6-1. Troubleshooting Questions to Solve Common Virtual Session Problems

Feature	Common Problems and Possible Resolutions
Get Started	
Roles	• What are the different roles in my platform? • Did the correct invitations with the correct link go to the right people for the role? • How are roles assigned? • How are the roles changed or moved in the session? • What are the different features and capabilities for each role?
Audio	If using a teleconference : • Is the teleconference provided by the platform or another party? • Do the attendees dial into the teleconference or do they enter their number into a form to receive a call back? • How do the attendees receive the information on how to join the teleconference? (For example, by pop up, email in advance, or posted in the session.) • Is the phone number listed separately from their name? Suggest they hang up and call back in. Or merge their name to their number or ask them to enter their attendee or participant ID number when they dial in. Note that not all systems accept entering the ID number after they have joined, so they may need to hang up and start again anyway. If using computer audio (VoIP): • Have they connected using the proper equipment: headphones, headsets, air pods, a microphone, or earbuds? • Is the privilege to speak enabled? • Have they asked for permission to speak? • Are they unmuted?
Participant List (including attention tracking)	• Where is the participant list located and who can view it? • What indicators or icons are on the participant list to help you determine how people are connected: mobile, web client, strength of connection, and so on? • Can the participant list be minimized, collapsed, expanded, moved, repositioned, or resized? • Is attention tracking enabled, if needed?
Webcam	• Is your webcam compatible with your platform? • Have you exited, restarted, and rejoined the session? • Has your platform recognized or initialized your webcam? • Is your background, angle, and lighting ready for you to be seen on webcam? • Do you know exactly when you are on and off camera? Check the view settings.

Feature	Common Problems and Possible Resolutions
Recording	• Was the recording feature enabled and will both the audio and the visual be included? • Did you have the correct role to control the starting, pausing, stopping, and saving of recordings? • Where did the recording get saved? • Is the file type compatible with participant systems? • Is the recording link password protected? • In what other ways can the recording be shared? For instance, can it be downloaded or sent as a link? • Can you track who is watching the recording?
Basic Interaction	
Feedback	• Does the platform include feedback icons? • Are the feedback tools enabled? • Do the participants know they can use feedback icons, and if so, where they are located? • Is the presenter asking people to use and pay attention to the feedback feature?
Chat	• Have the attendee chat privileges been set? (Note the difference between public vs. private, and so on.) • Does everyone know where chat is located? • Does everyone know how to use chat and what is expected of them? • Is the presenter paying attention to the chat, or do they have someone assisting them?
Whiteboard	• Does the platform have a whiteboard, and if so, do you know how to share one? • Once a whiteboard is shared, do you know how to return to the prepared content? • What is the best way to save the whiteboard (for example, platform feature or screen capture)? • Can uploaded or shared files be annotated upon and used as a whiteboard?
Annotation Tools	• Does the platform have annotation or drawing tools? • Where are they located? • Can they be enabled for the participants? • Can the annotations be edited, moved, cleared, and saved?
Share File	• Is share file the intended way of showing the file, rather than sharing it via its source application? • Is the file type compatible with your platform? • Is the file size supported? • Are the fonts in your image compatible? • Do you need to make the slide an image so that the individual images in it do not "move" when they get covered during the upload?

Feature	Common Problems and Possible Resolutions
Share Screen	• Oversharing: Has the presenter shared too much and accidentally shown something unintended for the audience? For example, it is advisable to close instant messaging applications. • Under-sharing: Has the presenter shared their screen, but no one can see it? • Cannot share: Does the presenter have the right role and permission to do it? • Screen frozen: Try taking the presenter role back and ask the presenter to restart and rejoin. • Unintended sharing: If an attendee shared when they were not asked to share, then they might have too many permissions.
Advanced Interaction	
Polling	• Was the poll created and attached in advance? • Do you have the role necessary to manage the poll? • Do you need to close the poll before the results can be shared? Check the format of the shared results. • Did you save the results?
Notes	• Is the notes feature enabled, or is the notes pod or panel in view? • Has a designated note taker been chosen, or will each participant take their own notes? • Have the proper privileges been set? • Have the notes been saved?
Q&A	• Is there a designated area for participants to ask questions that is different from chat? • Do the participants know where to find the Q&A panel or pod? • Do you have the roles identified and assigned to the people who need to manage Q&A?
File Transfer	• Does this feature exist within your platform or need to be enabled? • Is there a file size or file type restriction? • Does the file get a designated location or is it sent via the chat? • How exactly do participants take and receive the files?
Breakout	• Does the platform have a breakout feature? • Is the audio going to follow the attendees in and out of the breakout rooms? • How will participants communicate with the leaders once they are in a breakout room? • Can the leaders visit the breakouts rooms? • Can the work be saved or shared once the participants return?

Designing, Preparing, Partnering

Designing Materials With Production Details

In This Chapter

○ A three-step design process for virtual success
○ Three ways to document who does what, when, and how
○ Visual production details and instructions to assist attendees

The two most important parts of having a plan in place when producing a live online session are managing the *what* and the *when*: what technical tasks need to be managed, and when should they be addressed? I've delivered hundreds of virtual training sessions, online meetings, and webinars, and every time I am with a live audience it is so easy to lose track of the technical details as I focus on my attendees. I forget I have polls to run and annotation tools to enable, and even if I am working with another person to help with these tasks, they too need to know the what and the when. Having designed a plan for these specific details helps me deliver a more focused and engaging session.

When more than one person is responsible for the successful production of an online session, notes on how things will run are important for clarity and organization. In order to remember and refer to all that you have learned about the platform and the plans that have been put in place to produce your session, having a clear and usable set of materials to follow will keep the producer, the presenter, and the attendees organized and on track. Participants are often confused about how to use the features of the platform properly, so providing them with instructions on-screen and details in handouts is an excellent way to minimize any problems. Additionally, having a clear outline for the host and presenter on who does what, how, and when will keep everyone in alignment, ensuring nothing is missed during the live delivery of the session.

Whichever instructional design theory and process are used to develop the content of your program, the tasks for the live virtual delivery of the session will be essentially the same. Webex, Zoom, Adobe Connect, and so on are the delivery method, acting as a physical space or room does, informing how things move, act, and feel, but not directly deciding the goals, objectives, and content that is being shared. The approaches and theories used to design your content still apply virtually, and referring to the information, processes, guidelines, and examples in this chapter will help you make the most of your live online experiences, no matter your instructional design approach.

Materials such as presenter notes, outlines, facilitator and participant guides, and even PowerPoint slides will help you manage the session if the platform unexpectedly stops working while you are live. Asking participants to refer to their handouts and provided content while conducting the session via teleconference is one way to proceed if the platform and the computer interface go down. It's typically the case with today's technologies that they will not stay down for long, allowing everyone to reconnect or automatically reconnecting them within a short period of time. Requesting attendees refer to handouts, resources, and other materials that have been shared with an them in advance and conducting a conversation with them via a teleconference until the platform is up and running again is an excellent way to stay on schedule and keep people engaged.

When conducting a small online meeting, it may not be necessary to provide materials or create a fully documented plan on how to technically run the meeting. Keeping it simple with an agenda and a few notes on which features to use during the meeting is likely enough. For example, include notes on the PowerPoint slides to remind yourself to enable annotation tools for collaboration on a whiteboard or to use chat to capture ideas from a brainstorm. If the meeting is a large online, all-company meeting where multiple presenters will be involved and many attendees will be joining in, it is a best practice to have a documented plan, shared by all who are leading the meeting, so everyone is clear on how things will work.

Three-Step Design Process for Virtual Success

To design the flow of interactions and learning activities for your large online meeting, webinar, and virtual instructor-led training sessions, follow this three-step process. Begin by clearly outlining the why, the who, and the how for your program or session. This design process is especially useful for determining how to convert traditional in-person training into the virtual instructor led environment. It serves as a guide for what needs to be included, for what purpose, how many people, how much time, and what features of the platform to use.

1. **Identify the Goal and Objectives**
   What needs to be accomplished and what does that look like?
2. **Determine What's Social**
   Which objectives are best completed with other people together at the same time?
3. **Map the Interactions to the Features**
   Which features of your live online platform allow those interactions?

1. Identify the Goal and Objectives

What needs to be accomplished and what does that look like? What is the purpose of the webinar or training session, and what are the specific things the participants will do once they have completed the session? It's important to be clear on the point of your session to avoid an ineffective lecture or an uninteresting reading of PowerPoint slides.

It is also a good practice to make your point clearly on actions that participants will take rather than just assuming what you present is for their "understanding." For instance, "Attendees will be updated on our newest products," versus "Attendees will be able to list the latest features and benefits of our newest products." The clearer the objective, the easier it is to decide what to present live online and exactly how to do it in a way that engages participants. It also helps identify what should be done in other formats such as independent reading, recordings, discussion boards, microlearning, and all the other learning approaches available.

2. Determine What's Social

Which objectives are best completed with other people together at the same time? Look back through each of the objectives of your presentation or training. To determine what should be delivered live online, choose the objectives that will be best learned with people participating at the same time. Some objectives will be best experienced together, such as creating a new process or brainstorming ideas, while others will be slightly more difficult, such as reviewing leading practices or outlining specific steps in a process. Sometimes it is less about the program's learning objectives and more about the need to bring a group of peple together for other reasons, such as team bonding or communication strengthening. Ultimately, the decision is made based on your organizational goals, the needs of your participants, and the availability of time and technologies. Focusing on the objectives where people will have a better experience learning together will produce the most impact.

In addition to writing books, I teach trainers how to be live online virtual trainers. An obvious objective of the program is to master the virtual classroom technology. As part of this, I do not walk through the steps of how to use each feature in a live online session with all participants present. Instead, I train using all the features I can in each session, providing a model of how each feature can be used as a form of inspiration. Each participant is then given an independent assignment to open their own virtual classroom session, in their own platform, walking through each feature on their own. We then regroup in another live session to review and pose questions.

It would be a waste of participants' time to maintain a social component by having them in the live virtual session watch me click around or watching each other. Instead, I've designed the activity to be done independently, while they can learn together during the review. This leaves participants inspired by the possibilities available to them with the features of the platform and able to use the features of the platform to create engaging learning experiences themselves.

3. Map the Interactions to the Features

Which features of your live online platform allow the desired interactions? The difficult analysis work is complete; now you need to determine which features of the platform to use. Whatever the choice—whiteboard, chat, webcam, breakout—it simply needs to support and encourage the social interactions and learning objectives of the session. After exploring all that your platform has to offer, you'll likely have an idea of what kinds of experiences you want to create.

A helpful guideline: When they need to type long sentences, use chat, and when they could circle, point, or choose things, consider a whiteboard or an annotated slide. The same types of interactions can be done in breakouts, and by adding discussions, webcams, software usage, and website explorations, there are many choices for you to create interaction as well as collaboration in your live online meetings, webinars, and virtual classroom training sessions.

Consider what you would do if you needed to conduct a brainstorm. I find using the chat feature to be the most effective way to facilitate this discussion. Participants usually have more than one word to type and using their keyboards in chat is more comfortable than a text tool on a whiteboard. For a pros versus cons brainstorm activity, it's easy to organize the chat by typing PROS first, and asking participants to provide their responses. Once they have responded, type CONS next as a divider, and ask participants to follow with responses. All the messages can be saved and referred to later, or even reviewed in the moment using a scrolling feature.

As a second example, I like to develop a slide with space for annotating when debriefing an activity. The centralized visual serves as a place to focus without being distracted. I often type key words as participants take turns talking and it helps everyone focus and listen as the words appear.

Documenting Who Does What, When, and How

There are many details to recall when presenting a webinar or delivering a training, both in-person and live online. In-person is likely more familiar, and most people have confidence that they will effectively manage all that needs to be done given their previous experience. Yet, presenters and trainers for in-person sessions still create presentations, lesson plans, activities, and resources ahead of time to stay on schedule, on topic, and in tune with participant needs and expectations. Delivering live online sessions is no different when it comes to the topic and participant needs, but it is vastly different in that the physical space becomes a virtual one, requiring the use of technology to manage the entire experience.

How, after all the hard work of using the three-step process to design the live online session, does this get documented clearly and usefully for delivering live to an audience? It's important that this documentation can be easily referenced while providing technical support at the same time. Things move quickly when presenting online, and if there are too many words, or too many details, they tend to get ignored and go unused. But it remains crucial to have a plan documented for the delivery of a webinar or a virtual instructor-led training so you can remember what needs to be done during each segment. And if you are partnering with someone who is likely at their own computer in an entirely separate location, then the documentation is even more valuable.

It's necessary to plan each segment of the session from the moment it opens until the close. What's being shown, what's being said, how the technology is being used, how much time is needed, and who is doing each of these things all need to be determined. And, it needs to be easy to use, ideally referenced at a glance, so that the focus remains on the experience of the online session. There are several ways to do this; listed next are three approaches that work well.

PowerPoint Notes

Using the notes section of PowerPoint works well for small online meetings and uncomplicated webinars, where presenting, chatting, and polling comprise the extent of the interactions planned. Drafting a version of the script, adding key points as needed, and indicating what to do technically will help you stay on track and communicate to anyone else with whom you may be working. See Figure 7-1 for an example of what this may look like.

Figure 7-1. Introductory Slide for a Webinar

Virtual Facilitator and Producer Guide

In all the years I've been designing, delivering, and producing live online training, webinars, and meetings, I've tried many different formats for documenting the plan, but none has been more effective and useful than the one I learned from my mentor and friend, Nanette Miner, the Training Doctor. It remains my preferred format for all the virtual classroom instructor materials I develop, and I remain grateful for her guidance and encouragement early in my virtual training career.

Her template is effective because the simple layout manages not only content and technology, but also the timing of exactly who does what and when. I have always appreciated that important detail because we've all attended webinars when links were sent in chat for participants who were not ready for them, or breakouts were launched before the instructions on what to do in them were explained. It's details such as these that differentiate a well-planned, intentionally designed online delivery from one hastily pulled together using the same processes and materials from a similar in-person program.

Space is provided for scripted content for the facilitator and the producer, and there is also room for bulleted key points or extra instructions. Importantly, space is provided for the technology and any production tasks, and in such a way that the timing is clearly indicated based on their position in the column.

The template itself is primarily a three-column table: an image of the visuals, the facilitator's script and instructions, and the production tasks and platform details. This template works even when not using a designated person as a producer as it separates the technical details from the content details. For instance, in the case of a breakout activity, the facilitator column would contain the setup for the small group activity including instructions and details on what needs to be accomplished. Also included would be ideas on what to expect as a result of the activity and how to properly debrief it once the participants return. The producer (technical) column would indicate details on how many breakout rooms to set up, how much time to allot, and what materials to load into each one, if applicable. Scripting may be included, but if it is similar each time, it is best to create a seperate file for repeated use.

The same principle applies to any step-by-step technical instructions for the features. Create a separate document for things that remain the same. This is efficient for the instructional design team and creates a master file that can stay current with software updates and changes to the interface.

The template in Figure 7-2 is used with permission from Nanette Miner. And following the template in Figure 7-3 is an example activity from one of my actual learning activities, One Word, from my Online Virtual Facilitator Certificate.

Also consider this story from Nanette on the importance of design for virtual production: "I can't emphasize enough the importance of the header information at the start of each new topic or segment of your facilitator guide. I learned this lesson the hard way when sitting in on a course I had designed, which was being taught by someone else and the trainer started drawing unintended conclusions from the activity. I thought to myself, 'Where the heck is she going with this?'

"Then, like any good trainer, I realized that if the learners don't do what you expected, 99 percent of the time it is because you gave poor instructions—so I examined why she did not understand the purpose of the activity and realized that it was because I had not made it clear. Without that direction she was left to draw her own conclusions and fill in the blanks. From that point on I added the short overview you see in Figure 7-2 to every facilitator guide I've created."

Figure 7-2. Sample From Nanette Miner's Facilitator and Producer Guide Template

Timing: 10 minutes *before* official start		**Tools:** List any tools or methodology used, such as Annotation, Poll, Discussion
Overview: Give a brief overview of what is happening during this time, such as: *The Warmup is intended to get learners focused on the topic and used to engaging with the technology, the facilitator, and one another.*		
Slide or Media	**Facilitator**	**Producer/Technical**
Re-size picture to 2.1 wide; height will self-adjust		
	TRANSITION: Start the transition text here. Put one more carriage return after the last line of text.	
	TRAINER'S NOTE: Copy this row and drop it in the table where you need it. Delete this row if unneeded. (10 point font—intentionally)	

Figure 7-3. My Example of a Facilitator and Producer Guide Template

Timing: 5 minutes
Tools: Presentation, Annotation, Audio

Overview: Gain insight into what is most likely a negative response to a single word and some of what the online trainer must overcome to engage a virtual audience.

Note: The ASK on page 2 is the most important part of this activity. Be sure to make time for it.

Also note: You may not change the slides or the materials for this assignment, but please use the script as a guide, making the words your own so that it is a natural delivery. I'm not expecting you to read it word for word, but I am expecting the messaging to be the same.

Slide	Facilitator or Trainer	Producer (Technical)
WEBINAR	SAY: Let's take a moment to reflect on how people react to words, specifically one word that is often used in our industry to mean online learning. *Advance slide.* ASK: What is your experience with the word you now see on this slide? Type your response using your annotation tools, anywhere in the open space. Don't forget to add your name. And please use the green check or thumbs up to signal when you are done. *WAIT for 75% green checks or thumbs up before commenting.* Look for answers like: • Boring • Time waster • Lecture • Convenient • Technical problems	ASSIST participants with the text tool if necessary. WATCH for ideas that might come in chat.

	CALL on 2 people, 1 minute per person QUICKLY COMMENT ON • Biases and commonalities • How much we must overcome to make it a positive experience in attendees' minds • The positive answers too ASK: (Important!) As virtual facilitators: What can we learn from these reactions? Raise your hand. Call on 1 person, 1 minute Alternative: If time is short, ask them to respond using chat instead of using annotation tools. Comment on a few, call on at least 1 person to explain.	USE annotation tools to highlight or circle points referred to
TRANSITION	Participants often have a negative reaction when they hear the word "webinar" for a learning session that is based on prior unfortunate experiences. We have much to overcome to win them all over, and yet I'm certain with all your new skills that you are up for the challenge!	

Session Checklist

A third method of documenting who does what, when, and how is to develop a session checklist, commonly used by a vendor who provides production services. Working with a vendor is an excellent way to get the support and technical expertise needed to ensure your webinars and virtual classroom training sessions are successful without having to formally employ a person in the role, or create additional tasks for existing employees. Working with such vendors requires information to be shared with them on how you expect the session to run and the content you intend to share. Companies such as the Virtual Learning Collaborative help individuals and organizations create engaging learning experiences by partnering with them to deliver live online sessions. The session checklist I have used with them has been easy to use, efficient, and effective for communicating to the producers.

Their session checklist includes information like the title, date, time, and duration. Also listed is both the producer's and presenters' or instructor's contact information including emails, phone numbers, instant messaging names, and backup mobile phone numbers. Important platform information includes the links, logins that will be used during live delivery, and technical information such as whether the session will be recorded. And finally, there is an area for additional notes and special information such as info on extra presenters, or other instructions that will affect the delivery of the session.

Once the general information about the session is documented, the session is listed chronologically according to the slide numbers or other visuals presented. This list is then used by the producer, making it their responsibility to follow along and perform as the session is delivered. Such a checklist is easy to follow and quick to put together. It helps planners and designers of sessions be clear on what is happening each moment throughout the sessions. Though the checklist is focused primarily on the production tasks and platform management, there is room for notes and extra tips as needed. The content script is not included in a checklist such as this, so presenters and trainers should use either the formal facilitator's guide as mentioned before or notes in PowerPoint slides if the session is not too complicated.

See Figure 7-4 for a sample of what was included in a VLC session checklist for one of my two-hour live online workshops, called Interact and Engage! Activities for Spectacular Live Online Events.

Sonia Furini, owner of Virtual Learning Collaborative, has this to say about session checklists: "A session checklist paves the way to success in our producer's preparation of their duties in the virtual classroom. Not everyone understands the need for a checklist or that such a thing exists! We work with our clients to provide a thorough overview of the many benefits of checklists, and then we move forward in assisting them to develop this resource. The session logistics, contact information, and required tasks are invaluable components of a well-developed checklist. We always work with one to ensure the best outcomes!"

Figure 7-4. Example Session Checklist for Producer Activities

Slide #	Producer Activity
Participant Manual	Please have the .pdf of the PM open and add page numbers in the chat as we go along.
Pre-Session	Join me 15 minutes ahead of time–it's fine! z-Kassy2 is my second computer and it can remain in the role of attendee. We will Webcam! Breakout Activity at the end: 4 people max–random assignments are OK.
Pre-Session	Please monitor chat the whole time–add in and keep the conversation going! I love it! Raise your hand to let me know if you want me to notice something that I missed and any time you want to talk and add in actually! Add notes from key things that I and participants say into the chat too.
6	I have prepared a poll here that I will launch.
8	If requested, explain annotation tools. This is where we will teach them for the first time how to annotate. When they type, ask them to add their names next to their entries. I will call on them to talk. Save a screenshot of the slide for me as a backup.
10	Participants will be chatting. I will call on them to speak.
18	Participants will type their names on the slide. They will then use chat to type the number and why. I will call on a few to share.
21	Participants will type on the slide. I will ask a few to share–maybe even show on webcam, depending.
25	Just a quick call out to mention that the details are in their PM on page 8. We are not going to do it as I will just describe it.
27	I will explain and then call on them to share how it is connected to an activity they do. I will likely have them raise hand and talk; we'll see how it is going.
HEADS UP!	BREAKOUTS COMING SOON! TEAMS OF NOT MORE THAN 4. RANDOM ASSIGNMENT IS FINE.
30-32	Scavenger Hunt! Send the link AtlasObscura.com after I reveal it on the slide. The attendees will answer all three questions on their own and write them down in their participant manual on page 23. I will ask them to raise their hand once they have all three answers. We will wait for three people to raise their hands. I will call on the first person to answer over the audio. If they get it wrong; we move to the next person. Winner gets a book; I will need their mailing address. Ask them to chat it to you to give to me.

Figure 7-4. Example Session Checklist for Producer Activities (cont.)

Slide #	Producer Activity
35	Participants will raise their hand to volunteer. I will ask two to annotate as they talk through their story, connecting the images with a line or something.
39-41	Breakout! In teams of not more than four, they will discuss the 10 lessons on page 14. Each team discusses it in a group and then shares one action item when we return. I'd really love to have at least 15 minutes for this activity and will plan for it. This activity is the ending—the rest is a wrap up and call for questions.

Production Details for the Audience

The development of materials thus far has been focused on the perspective of the hosts, trainers, presenters, and other session leaders, but what about the participants? What will help them be successful connecting to and participating in your live online session? Chapter 8 is focused on strategies and techniques to fully prepare attendees for participating and learning in the live virtual environment, but support for that experience begins with the design of visual cues and instructions. Placing instructions and guidelines on PowerPoint slides and including technical instructions in handouts ensures you won't be reliant only on audio. People are not always listening, may have technical problems that cause their audio connection to cut out, and sometimes just don't hear things, so having details in other places is a leading practice. Use the following examples as guidelines when creating your materials.

Visual Cues

Participants do well with visual cues on slides that remind them which feature to use. Such cues also serve as a reminder to trainers and presenters! The slide in Figure 7-5 is an example of how to open a session and request participants use the features as soon as they connect. Placing instructions like this on the slide helps those who have not yet opened their audio connections to also begin participating in the session. Figure 7-6 shows a second example of a cue, this time not only alerting participants that there is a poll, but also reminding the presenter to refer to it.

Figure 7-5. Opening Activities Using Features

Figure 7-6. A Presenter's Reminder to Ask a Question Using the Polling Feature

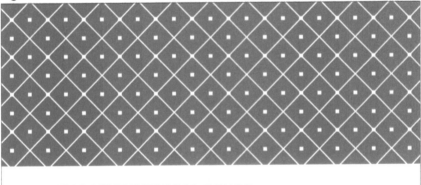

Instructions

Virtual attendees need instructions to participate in specific activities and to be successful in the virtual environment in general. When sending participants to another application—for example, to search a website or to work on a spreadsheet to do an assignment—they will need to know how to navigate back to the virtual classroom's main window. When placing participants into breakout rooms to work together in small groups, it is easy for them to get lost or be confused on how to work in that new environment. Note that participants moving to breakout rooms for the first time may be nervous about it, thus more concerned with that than the actual assignment, so be sure to provide clear instructions at the moment of need.

In Figures 7-7 and 7-8, participants are performing a website scavenger hunt that requires them to look for answers on a website and then compete to finish first. They need the link, instructions to document their answers including the page number, and directions to indicate they are ready and to speak when called upon. Figure 7-7 shows the slide used, and the accompanying participants manual references are shown in Figure 7-8.

In Figures 7-9 and 7-10, participants are working in small groups to review what they have learned during the session using the Geometric Close. It is helpful to have content instructions separate from technical directions, so note the use of a T chart format to organize the two. Figure 7-9 is of the slide in the virtual classroom, and Figure 7-10 is a copy of what is in the printed participant manual. Note how the technical instructions are repeated in the manual.

Last, consider the breakout example script that appears in Figure 7-11 for how to explain and manage breakouts with participants.

Figure 7-7. Website Scavenger Hunt Slide

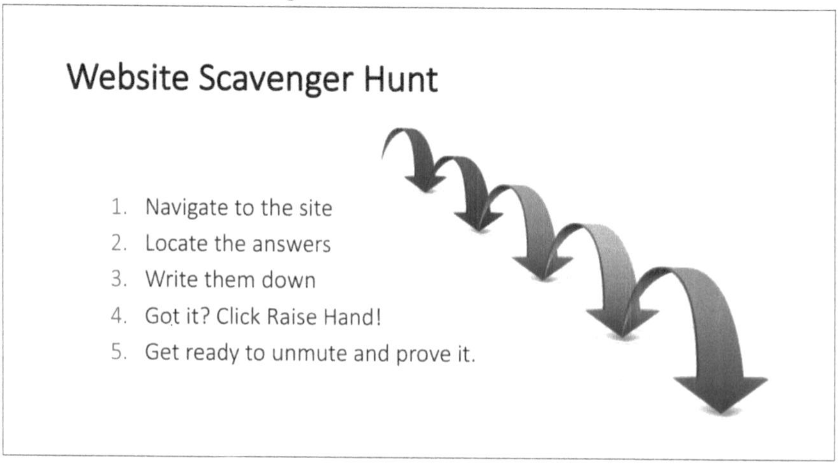

Figure 7-8. Website Scavenger Hunt Participant Manual

Website Scavenger Hunt

Activity Instructions:

1. Go to the link posted in the chat to search and locate the answers.

2. Write them down here.

3. Got it? Raise your hand.

4. Get ready to prove it!

Question	Answer
Look on the screen for the questions!	

Figure 7-9. Final Session Breakout Activity Slide

A GEOMETRIC CLOSE

ACTIVITY

- Wait for us to load the file **S1_Learnings.ppt**
- Discuss your "key learnings" from today's session
- Take turns, each person choosing one shape / question to answer

TECHNICAL

- Click Yes to Start/Join Breakout Room
- Presenter? Start the conversation.
- Place pointer, type notes
- Be prepared to discuss once we regroup
- Click *Ask for Help* if needed

Figure 7-10. Final Session Breakout Activity Participant Manual

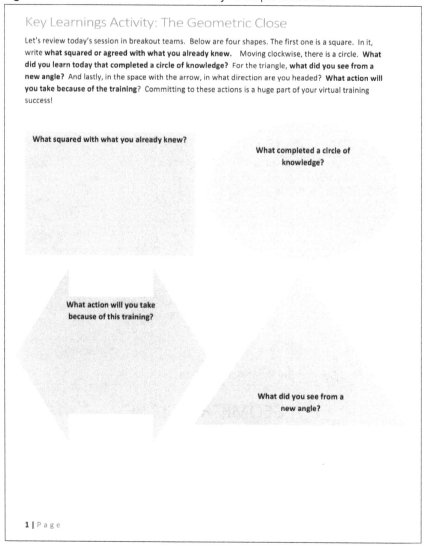

Key Learnings Activity: The Geometric Close

Let's review today's session in breakout teams. Below are four shapes. The first one is a square. In it, write **what squared or agreed with what you already knew.** Moving clockwise, there is a circle. **What did you learn today that completed a circle of knowledge?** For the triangle, **what did you see from a new angle?** And lastly, in the space with the arrow, in what direction are you headed? **What action will you take because of the training?** Committing to these actions is a huge part of your virtual training success!

What squared with what you already knew?

What completed a circle of knowledge?

What action will you take because of this training?

What did you see from a new angle?

1 | P a g e

Conclusion

Whether designing a virtual learning session, organizing a meeting, or presenting a webinar, it is important to be clear on who does what, when, and how. So many of these details may seem to be for the people leading the session, but as we saw, it is also valuable for the attendees. Providing written and visual details like what to do, where to look, and how to participate will help keep everyone engaged. Given how much is expected of attendees, let's now examine how best to prepare them to successfully engage in a live online session.

Reflection Questions

▶ Which part of the three-step virtual design process resonates with you and why?

▶ Which ideas from the three ways to document who does what, when, and how will you likely use the most?

▶ What ways will you add visual cues to your slides for your attendees?

Figure 7-11. Breakout Example Script

Producer: SAY	Technical: DO
In a moment we'll be working in breakout groups. Please raise your hand if you are ready.	Wait for the raised hands. If someone does not click on their raise hand button, gently call on them by name. Do not dwell here if they do not respond. Adjust breakout assignments as needed.
Additional notes: 1. Should you assign the stepped away participant to a breakout group or leave them in the main room? Use your best judgment based on the breakout scenario at hand. • If you need to adjust your breakout assignments, ask the trainer to refresh everyone on the scenario while you do so. 2. Don't to spend too much time over-explaining the breakout process.	
Each breakout group has an assigned presenter who will be the first to receive an invite. Presenters are [state names of your assigned presenters]. Click YES and the breakout will start. Once the presenter has started the breakout, the other team members will receive their invites to join. Team members, click YES once more to join your breakout.	It is recommended to take everyone off mute before starting the breakout.

Figure 7-11. Breakout Example Script (cont.)

Producer: SAY	Technical: DO
Let's unmute and get started! OK everyone, please click yes! Once you are in your breakouts, introduce yourselves to each other and (if applicable) I will be in shortly to load your assignment.	UNMUTE ALL START BREAKOUTS Watch as they all join their respective breakout groups. Help if needed. When loading slides in the breakout rooms–DO NOT join audio. Instead, have your trainer join the groups on audio if there is concern. Enter the room, take the ball, load the slides, return the ball, and exit. Only once you've loaded slides for each breakout group should you return, join audio, and guide them with further instructions or assistance. When ending breakouts, broadcast a message and then click End Breakouts, which will trigger the 30-second delay. The participants will all be returned to the main room. Now invite each breakout presenter to share content, if applicable.
PRO TIP! Alternatively, you can end breakouts by entering each room, telling the group that we're coming back, taking the ball, and ending the breakout. This will also give you a chance to take a snapshot of the assignment they worked on, which you can then load in the main room during debrief. This is recommended if you have the time and believe that it will be beneficial. Use your best judgment.	

This script is used with Webex Training Center and adapted from Joe Murray, Digital Operations Manager at Dale Carnegie Training.

Preparing Attendees to Participate

In This Chapter

○ The consequences of the unprepared attendee
○ Steps and examples to prepare attendees technically and emotionally
○ Helping attendees stay accountable for their own success

What separates passive attendees and active participants? Understanding the difference between the two can determine whether your virtual session becomes a success or a flop. Ultimately, attendees who are technically and emotionally prepared to engage online are ready to be full participants in any live virtual session.

The problem is that attendees often do not know how to properly attend a live online session, let alone use all the features of the platform to communicate and learn. They know how to be and act in a classroom or in the office because they learned it long ago when they first attended school and had it reinforced through the workplace. Fast forward to now and people are being given links to join sessions without any clue on how to act once they get there. They do not know the technology well enough and usually only focus on trying to get their computers to work without giving thought to how they should conduct themselves once they arrive.

Why a Lack of Preparation Can Derail the Session

Far too many online meetings are fraught with technical problems stemming from the attendee's inability to join from their computers or devices or connect to the audio portion of the session without disrupting everything. The basics of any online meeting platform require a solid internet connection and some form of audio that will not pick up background noise or interference from the device being used. So many attendees do not know these basics and are surprised when they click a meeting link to find that they may need to allow the platform access to their computer for things to work. Also, expecting to be able to speak using the built-in microphones and speakers on a laptop or mobile device without echoes, feedback, and other background noise is a common mistake.

Attendees also don't realize how much the disruptions they cause for themselves also affect others. When webinars and virtual training and meetings start late due to a few who cannot log in smoothly, others are left waiting and waste time as focus is placed on those who need technical support. Additionally, when someone attending doesn't pay attention to whether they are muted or not, the entire conference hears them typing on their keyboards, talking to others, and in some cases doing things like placing orders for food! And when someone doesn't know how to manage the features to communicate, it slows down the conversation for the whole group. When trainers conduct collaborative learning sessions using breakouts, if attendees do not understand how to work together inside the breakout, time for the learning will be lost.

Due to confusion surrounding the technical side of just connecting to and being in an online session, attendees often will not be able to pay attention to and learn from the content. Otherwise simple instructions seem more confusing and trying to learn something like new software or business processes becomes more complicated because attendees need to navigate multiple windows or devices while learning online. It's hard to focus on the point of an activity if the process of beginning it is difficult.

It's no wonder then that people are hesitant to lead and attend live online training. There must be better way!

Attendees need to become knowledgeable and confident participants by learning how to properly be in a live online session, both technically and emotionally. And it's on all of us organizing and leading online sessions to step up and figure how best to manage these problems and help not only the attendees, but also ourselves to be more successful online. We must prepare them. Just sending an email about system and technical requirements is not working. Expecting participants to know how to act in a live online session without modeling it and reviewing it is not working. We have been trying these techniques for a couple decades, yet the problems persist. Let's examine what actions producers of virtual sessions can take to ensure participants are successful in attending and engaging in the sessions that have been meticulously designed and prepared for them.

Before the Session

Everything covered in this book up until now is relevant for understanding exactly what is required of participants to make the technology work. As you have learned what it takes for you to plan, learn, and run a live online session, you have also been learning exactly what is needed for participants. But communicating this to them—and making sure they have all they need so they know how to make it all work—is a different story. Let's review specifically what they need before the virtual session, all in one place, so you can prepare participants to properly participate. That is your mantra: prepare participants to properly participate!

Ask Participants to Prepare Their Physical Environment

Participants need to attend from a place where they can focus on what is happening and be involved as requested. If the session is a large webcast or webinar where the attendees are in listen-only mode, they simply need a comfortable place from which they can listen, watch what is being presented, and perhaps respond to a poll or send in a question as requested. But what about a virtual meeting or live online training session?

If attendees are expected to participate in a virtual session, they will need to be in a comfortable and quiet location, connected to their audio via computer or telephone, and on a stable internet connection. The space around them will affect their own experience and that of the other attendees when they appear on camera and unmute themselves. Attendees should be aware of what and who is around them, so they do not create disruptions for themselves or others. Attending a live online training from your gate at the airport is simply not ideal: It's loud, it's likely not a stable internet connection, it's probably uncomfortable, and it will be cut short when you need to board or change gates. I'll never forget the time we had an attendee in one of our sessions who was trying to talk over the gate announcements! We finally asked him to just disconnect as it was disruptive to the rest of us. Another extraordinary situation was when from one attendee's unmuted audio connection we all heard, "Welcome to McDonald's, may I take your order?" We all requested cheeseburgers.

If attendees will be speaking over audio connections and appearing on camera, be sure to clearly communicate these details to them in advance. Many people view online learning as something that is done alone and from anywhere, but in the case of a live, interactive, and collaborative meeting or training, attendees will need to properly set up the physical space around them before they can effectively participate. It's so important to let attendees know this information ahead of time, and then it is equally important to hold them accountable for it. If someone joins the session from a noisy place or in any other way that will be disruptive or inconducive to the experience intended, ask them to rejoin properly, or at another time. We'll discuss more on this concept of accountability at the end of this chapter. Encourage participants to set up their offices and spaces with the following in place:

- A quiet space if speaking on audio
- A comfortable chair and desk from which to sit or stand for the duration of the session

- A professional background and surroundings if appearing on webcam
- Space and materials for taking notes on printed handouts
- Snacks and water or other drinks
- Do not disturb messages for the office door, email, and instant message programs

Have Participants Test Their Equipment, Software, and Connection

In all the cases previously listed, reliable and stable internet connections are required. A high-speed internet connection is essential for computer audio (VoIP) and webcam capabilities, and frankly is best for any online session. It is important to note that some people might not have much of a choice or didn't have the awareness ahead of time. Be sure to know your audience and their needs and work together to create positive solutions based on the requirements of the platforms, session guidelines, and each attendee's unique environment.

Every software platform has its own official system requirements listing details such as the type of computers or other devices to use, operating systems, browsers, and so forth. A simple internet search will take you to the list for each one. They can be a bit overwhelming to read and understand, so you may find it helpful to enlist the knowledge and skills of an IT professional.

What follows is a list of the basic equipment, software, and internet connectivity requirements that work with most live online meeting, webinar, and training software platforms available today. Communicating the basics to your attendees is usually enough to make connecting and participating in a session successful. Formal technical support is needed if the basics are not working, as it likely means their computer or connection is blocking the software, or that their equipment isn't compatible with the software you're using to deliver the session. Most platforms have a URL that will allow attendees to test their computers and connections in advance of a session. Locate the test meeting URL on your platform's site or do a simple internet search, such as "Platform name test meeting." Some examples of this are:

- zoom.us/test
- helpx.adobe.com/adobe-connect/using/connection-test-connect-meeting.html
- webex.com/test-meeting.html

Share these expectations with your audience.

Here's the physical equipment participants will need:

- **Computer:** Laptop or desktop
- **Mobile Device:** Phone or tablet using the appropriate application downloaded in advance
- **Headset, Air Pods, Or Another Device That Allows Listening and Sending Audio:** Note that microphones are required to send audio whether it is a teleconference or computer audio. Speakerphones are not recommended as they cause audio interference and pick up too much external noise. Using external speakers and microphones is not recommended as it may cause feedback.
- **Webcam:** Using one built-into a laptop is fine, although a separate webcam usually provides higher quality
- **Desk:** Seated or standing, and a comfortable chair if seated

Here's what participants should know about their software and internet connection:

- Download the meeting platform software for full functionality. Some platforms have a web-based version that will not require a download, but it is usually limited in feature functionality.
- Email is often used for communications.
- If participants need to work on their own or open files on their computers, they will need the software for those assignments.
- A high speed internet connection is critical; a hard-wired (ethernet) connection is best, but strong and consistent WiFi will usually work also.

Communicate and Get Ready

As mentioned, it is a leading practice to request participants test their connections before the session is scheduled to begin. They also need to set up their environments so they can be ready to participate and pay attention. Sending emails with the information they need, yet somehow not overwhelming them with too many details, is a challenging task. Here is a list of strategies for communicating ahead of time all that participants will need:

Documentation. Create documentation in the form of handouts and emails; the shorter and easier to read, the better. Put only key information in them like a program overview, dates and times, logistics, and the test meeting link. Consider making a job aid with a few pictures or examples of how best to set up their space that also includes recommendations on what equipment they should use. The appendix includes examples of emails and documents for reference and ideas.

Test links. Be sure to include test links in the documentation, but also make it clear this link is different from the one they will use to attend their class or session. Clearly state "TEST" versus "ATTEND."

Videos. A short video can be an effective form of not only communicating the expectations for the program, but also for letting participants see and hear your personality before the session begins. Keep the video to less than three minutes and cover the basics of the technical setup and the program expectations. Mention what features they will be using, as appropriate, such as webcams, audio, chat, annotations tools, and breakouts. Remind them to set up their physical space appropriately and to bring water and snacks. Refer them to the documentation, test links, and their invitation to the live test session.

Live test sessions. Live test sessions are the most effective way for teaching participants how to be in the live online environment. Choosing to only send a document on how to connect to the audio or listing out how to use the chat and annotation tools sometimes isn't enough. Documents, test links, and videos are helpful and supportive, but until people click on the actual link, join the session, connect to the audio, and use chat and the other interactive tools, they just do not really get it. I run my Learning Launch session (detailed later in this chapter) as an example of this, either scheduling a standalone 30-minute workshop for multi-session training programs, or as a quick 10-minute introductory opening segment. For meetings and webinars, I teach attendees how to use the tools at the moment we need them after having sent them the platform test meeting links provided by each of the vendors. Remember that those test links check the system and connection, but not the attendee's ability to use the features of the platform, which is the point of a "live" test session.

This is a classic example of the difference between knowing about something and doing something. Videos of how to use the features of all the online platforms are all over the internet. People simply do not learn how to send a chat, unmute themselves, annotate a slide, or be in a breakout until they do it in a real live session for themselves. Make that happen by running real live test sessions. Make it the first session, or the first part of the first session for all your programs, or make it its own session that is run on a regular schedule and clearly communicated as a prerequisite for any other live online session they attend.

During the Session

Once participants have their workspaces set up and all the equipment, software, and internet connections are in place, it is time to join and participate in the live online session. It is important to produce a smooth first impression and to set the tone for how to act the moment they begin to connect. You have communicated expectations, they have connected, and now you and they can set the "culture" of the session.

Establish a Comfortable and Effective Environment

A comfortable environment in an online session is crucial to the overall experience. How people are feeling and thinking about the session they are attending plays a huge role in how they respond to everything going on, both technically and in terms of how they learn. It may be the case that everything is technically working, but if a person cannot locate their mute button, they may feel too frustrated or embarrassed to pay attention to the content of the session. If a person is struggling to locate the chat, or turn on a webcam, they are no longer paying attention to the content or messaging of the session. And if a person is feeling any discomfort around the content, the technology will only worsen their attitude and potentially their ability to learn effectively.

Once participants are comfortable with the technology, it is important to focus on establishing the culture of the session: the behaviors, the way things are done, and the standards and guidelines for how to conduct oneself using the technology. The culture of my sessions is always that chat is public and viewed the same as unmuting and talking would be. I read chats to myself, and verbally respond to them as if what was typed into the chat was said out loud. This takes some getting used to by participating in the beginning of my sessions, and I am sensitive to how that might at first overwhelm some attendees. I often say in the beginning of my sessions, "I'm reading the chat everyone, look at what Betty typed. She makes a strong point! What do you think about it, Frank?" This guides them to the chat if they were not looking and helps them get used to reading and responding whether that be out loud, or by typing more in the chat. I'm helping them become part of the culture of my sessions.

Leaders and producers of online sessions should model the behaviors they expect of participants. Having clear audio and strong internet connections is a start, but they should also use the chat, nonverbal feedback icons, and webcams in the same ways they expect from participants. Set and make clear the expectations for being in the session, just as has been done for years for people attending in-person meetings or training: Arrive on time, wear appropriate attire, avoid distracting side conversations or phone calls, raise your hand to speak, and respect other people while they are speaking.

The Learning Launch

A kickoff to the online learning experience, or an introduction to the live online learning environment, is the most effective way to teach people how to be in the virtual session. Table 8-1 shows an outline and step-by-step guide for starting a live online training session so that it is effective from the beginning. It teaches the features in the moment they need them, and it lets trainers, presenters, and producers model the expected behaviors, so participants can communicate with ease throughout the entire session. Adjust the length of time spent on each section, and exactly which sections to focus on based on the type of online session being delivered. For example, with virtual instructor-led training, go through each part since it is likely a small group who needs to use all the features of the platform while learning. However, with a large webinar, it is likely only necessary to cover the chat, Q&A, and feedback tools.

The example Learning Launch here is for Zoom. Additional Learning Launch slides may be downloaded under the Resources section of my website at KassyConsulting.com. Simply change the screen shots for your platform, adjusting the wording to match the features you will be using.

Table 8-1. The Learning Launch

The Learning Launch is designed to be a quick overview of the communication tools of the online platform. Ten to 15 minutes is all it usually takes to run this, but you can make adjustments as necessary. Also make sure to ask questions related to the content of the program, and conduct introductions relevant to the audience. Omit covering features the participants will not be using.

	Introduction to the Learning Launch Make sure you have introduced yourself (webcam!) before beginning this segment. Tell them these next few minutes are to launch the learning today and to see how we will communicate while we are together online. Important: Get participants to do (click on and try) everything. Don't just talk about it.
	Arrange the screen Help them arrange their screens so they can see the chat, participants, webcams, and so on. Mention the Speaker and Gallery View for webcams. Mention View Options > Side-by-side view as a great choice.
	Locate the webcam Make sure they are clear on where the webcam is located, and they know how to turn it on and off. This is also a good time to experiment with the virtual background if you have it enabled on your site or profile.
	Communicate using chat Send a question in chat for them to answer, for example: As an ice breaker: What is your favorite place to vacation? As a topical question: What is one thing you want to learn today? Mention that chat is an important form of communication throughout the session and can be used at any time.

	Communicate using audio Make sure they click to mute and unmute, and optionally disconnect and reconnect. No need to leave the session! Tell a funny story about not being muted! Have them practice muting and unmuting and look at their name in the participant panel to see when their audio is and is not muted.
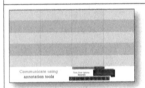	Communicate by giving feedback Click on all the feedback icons to see how they work and where they display when clicked. Ask them questions and have them reply using the feedback icons. Show them how to clear the icons themselves.
	Communicate using annotation tools Ask them to click View Options > Annotate > Text tool. Type their names to choose a spot–move them with your select tool, as needed. This is a good way to do introductions. I like to ask for: • Name • Role • Company or Department (if internal) • Location • One word that describes how they are feeling about the topic of today's session. Call on a few people to explain their one word (but be careful of timing).
	What's next and wrap up If this is a standalone session, then fill this with information and let them know what to do next. Or, transition to your agenda and begin the class.

Accountability

So, with all that is required of us to communicate to participants so they can be successful, what do we do when they don't show up properly? How do we handle it when they don't get the information in enough time, don't have time or resources, or simply cannot make any of it work no matter how hard they have tried?

The first and most important principle is to give people the benefit of the doubt. Treat them with respect and assume they have done and are doing their best. If they just enrolled in your course, or were late registrants to a webinar, they may not have had enough time to receive all the advance information, or other life circumstances may have interfered. Approach people with kindness and respect and do your best to help them in their moment of need, without interrupting the session for the others who have made it work and have shown up prepared.

If things are not working, or if the person cannot participate, be sure to not let that interfere with the experience for the other participants. Ask them to come back to the next session, or to seek the help they need from their local technical support team, or from you if you can provide it after the session you are currently leading is over. Provide people a safe place to communicate problems, but also require they be respectful of your time as well as the time of the others attending the session.

I always take care to communicate information ahead of time, both technically and about the topic and experience. I send emails, make videos, run live test meetings, and open all my sessions early. It is from there that I hold people accountable. When they choose not to read, watch, attend, or join early and then have problems or are confused, it is their responsibility to go back and take advantage of all the resources I have provided. Once it is the start time, and all the other attendees are ready to proceed, it is now my responsibility to be accountable to those who have followed the instructions and taken care of everything. On more than one occasion I have had to reiterate this to some attendees. I proceed and let them know they can go back and catch up, perhaps having to re-enroll and attend the next round of sessions once they are prepared. I follow up when it is acceptable and continue to offer the same help to them that was offered the others, but not once it is session start time.

Additionally, hold people to high standards. Communicate expectations as recommended and then hold attendees accountable for their own experiences. Notice when people join, greet them, and require they prove things are working by asking questions that need to be answered over the audio. Let them unmute and respond and ask them to use the chat and feedback tools also. Send them to breakout sessions and let them share their screens and whiteboards and save their work and share it when they return. The more we expect of them and let them do, the better they will be. They will learn how to do it and have more skills each time they participate. They will take these online meeting skills with them wherever they go, so in a sense, you are paying it forward for the next virtual trainer, online presenter, or webinar producer. Way to go!

Conclusion

Active participants need to be prepared to be present in the live online environment. While it is true that an audience may be passive due to the design of your session, the number of attendees, or the nature of the session, in other cases they may be passive because they simply are not ready or do not have everything they need to actively engage and be a part of all that you are asking of them. Prepare your attendees to participate and enjoy the level of engagement you can create in your live online sessions! In the next chapter, we'll look at how a facilitator and producer can best partner for success.

Reflection Questions

▸ Recall a time when one attendee's lack of preparation affected the experience for everyone else. What was your reaction? What was the reaction of the other attendees?

▸ What is the strangest place one of your attendees has joined a session from?

▸ What will you do to hold your participants accountable for their own experience?

Working Together in a Partnership

In This Chapter

- ○ The different types of producer roles and ways in which people work together
- ○ What are rehearsals and how are they managed?
- ○ Building strong working relationships

Throughout this entire book I've wanted to make clear the numerous production details that go into a successful online session. From planning the details, to learning the technology, and ultimately to live delivery, paying attention to the production tasks rather than focusing solely on the presentation and its content is what will differentiate your live online session from all the others being delivered around the globe every day. Depending on the nature of your session (meeting, training, or webinar), it is highly likely that working with another person in the official role of producer will be the most effective way to manage all the ancillary tasks associated with an engaging delivery. Some sessions, like sales or small team meetings, do not always require a high level of detail, but depending on the nature of the meeting and how many people are participating, assistance from another person focused on the technology might still be helpful.

However, working with another person can be challenging and sometimes confusing. How will you work together during a live session, who will do what exactly, and do you need to be physically in the same location to be successful? These are just a few of the concerns people have when considering working with another person to deliver an online session. Some concerns are logistical and tactical in nature, and others are about building a trusting and respectful relationship. Besides being able to address technical issues, producers need to execute the plan as well as skillfully manage the movement between segments of any program being delivered.

For example, if a session has several presenters on a panel, beyond preparing the presentation materials, questions, and polls for each presenter, a person managing the production tasks also needs cues on when to transition between presenters. Each presentation could have a different opening or special requests pertaining to their style and content. The person assisting as a producer would also need to manage the timing of each of these segments, keeping not only each presenter on track with all materials in place, but also remaining aware of all the participants and their needs throughout.

Most webinars and virtual classroom training sessions feature many moving parts, such as large audiences requiring technical support or planned detailed use of the live online platform features like breakout sessions. In either case, proper planning and partnership are essential to the successful delivery of the live session.

Technical and Facilitative Producers

If a person is going to be dedicated to fulfilling the production tasks of a live online session, then it is helpful to recognize that there are two types of producers, each with specific skills: technical and facilitative. Technical producers provide guidance and technical support on the use and management of the technology. They know the platform features and functions and are there to provide technical support throughout. Facilitative producers do all of this too, but they bring an additional set of skills to the session: They are also able to facilitate learning, present content, and guide participants through an engaging live online session if requested, in a secondary or back-up teaching role. They have also prepared themselves on the relevant content and have trainer and presenter skills for the live virtual environment.

Both webinars and live online training sessions require more focus on the technology than it takes to run an online meeting. However, producing a large webinar and supporting a live online training session are different. Trainers and presenters, whether working with a technical or a facilitative producer, need to make and share plans for the type of experiences that need to be delivered. People in the role of producer need to clearly understand the delivery plans to align the platform usage with the topic and the intended outcomes.

Webinars Typically Use Technical Producers

A technical producer's primary focus is the technical and logistical success of the session. They are not experts on content, but rather experts on managing the session itself, no matter the presenter.

I have presented at hundreds of webinars over the years, and it has increasingly become one of my favorite things to do as a consultant. For one, the topic of my presentations is typically virtual classroom training and webinar presenting, so it is enjoyable to be presenting on the very thing that is being done. Second, I enjoy the type of energy that a large crowd brings when they are engaged. I have appreciated the assistance producers have provided me while I was presenting, given that it is simply not realistic for me to take care of the logistical and technical needs of hundreds of participants while at the same time focusing on the timing and messaging of the presentation.

One of my favorite activities to do in a large webinar is a scavenger hunt where I send attendees to a website to find answers to several questions I have displayed on my presentation materials. The audience is often surprised that I am willing to send hundreds of people away from the main webinar screen, but with the help of a technical producer managing the chat to send the link, address technical problems, and help keep an eye out for the answers that come in via chat, I have found this activity to be highly engaging for attendees.

Webinar producers are the most commonly known and accepted type of producer, as the need for technical assistance is more obvious when there will be hundreds of attendees, not to mention all the marketing, registration, and communication effort it takes to deliver clear information to that many people. In fact, a team of not only a producer but also sales, product, marketing, and other supporting roles might be called on to assist with webinars. This does not change the fact that once a presenter is scheduled to speak at a webinar, they must partner with a producer to have an effective delivery.

Partnering with a webinar producer can be straightforward, but it can also create a feeling of loss of control for presenters if not managed carefully. Webinar producers are highly skilled individuals who usually work with multiple presenters at a time, managing several webinars in a day and likely many webinars in a week. The fact is most presenters are not skilled at managing the online platform. Thus, producers must not only run the live webinar and oversee the technical performance and management of it—they also teach the presenter how to use the designated web conferencing platform. It is, as you can imagine, a high-pressure role. As a result, webinar producers typically have a strict set of guidelines and expectations that presenters must follow that align with how the producer likes the webinar to run. If you are a presenter at a webinar working with a technical producer, you can likely expect the following (or if you are the one managing the production tasks, consider preparing and sending them):

- An email introduction confirming the date, time, and topic of your webinar as well as details on who your producer will be and an outline of expectations including whether a recording will be made of your webinar.

- Calendar invitations for a technical rehearsal and the live webinar, complete with the link and any other necessary technical requirements.
- A deadline request for submitting your presentation, handouts, polls, and any other planned interactions at least one week in advance of the webinar.
- A technical rehearsal or dry run that will test your computer, your internet connection, and your audio connection. It may also include a quick walk through of your content and, if needed, some training for you on how to use the features of the platform.
- A plan for how large the presentation should be, and how it will be shared in the webinar.
- A plan for how chat will be managed.
- A plan for how questions and answers will be managed and a request for any pre-planned questions that will be read out loud.
- A plan for how polls will be conducted, and a request for exactly when they should be launched. Usually there will be a request for a slide as a placeholder for each poll.
- A request to share contact information and backup plans for alternative connections should something go wrong on the day of the session.
- A reminder to join from the same computer, location, connection, hardware, and software that was used on the day of the dry run or technical rehearsal.
- A request to join the webinar at least 15–30 minutes in advance of the start time on the day of the session, including a final sound and system check.
- An announcement that there will be a recording if one is being made.
- A formal introduction before your presentation begins.
- A formal ending with wrap up agenda items, such as announcements, what to expect next, and a thank you.

Table 9-1 is an example of a plan sent to me by a webinar producer. If you are a presenter, this provides an idea of what will be expected of you. If you are a producer, you could use this as an example of a plan to send to a presenter.

Table 9-1. Example Plan From a Producer to a Presenter

TIME	ACTIONS
3:40 p.m. CET/ 9:40 a.m. EDT	Lynn open the session Kassy will show first slide of the deck: "Interact and Engage!"
3:52 p.m. CET/ 9:52 a.m. EDT	Kassy starts her countdown clock—10 min count down Lynn starts playing some fun music **Note: This countdown clock must be shown for the participants and us. Kassy, if your timer cannot be embedded on or in a full screen slide, then showing the timer exclusively (with no slide) is fine.
4 p.m. CET/ 10 a.m. EDT	**Lynn starts recording**
4:02 p.m. CET/ 10:02 a.m. EDT	Kassy moves to Slide 2 Lynn begins the webinar: • Introduces Kassy • Confirms recording • Explains how the session will be run, Q&A, etc.
4:05 p.m. CET/ 10:05 a.m. EDT	Kassy begins the session and runs her slides Lynn will chime in at times regarding chat comments and questions.
4:45 p.m. CET/ 10:45 a.m. EDT	Kassy finishes her session; Kassy and Lynn move to Q&A Lynn reads out the questions and Kassy answers
4:50 p.m. CET/ 10:50 a.m. EDT	Lynn starts prompting on chat for participants to complete the survey before leaving (will do so a few times)
4:58 p.m. CET/ 10:58 a.m. EDT	Kassy and Lynn finish Q&A Lynn gives a big THANK YOU to Kassy Lynn reminds participants of upcoming session; Slide showing upcoming session Lynn asks participants to complete survey; Slide showing survey: link to survey here Lynn reassures participants that they will get the handout, recording, and transcript: Slide showing THANK YOU

Virtual Classroom Training Typically Uses Facilitative Producers

Facilitative producers are those whose primary focus is the technical and logistical success of the training; they may also be skilled to teach segments of the class if needed, but in a secondary role to the trainer.

My first definition of a producer stems from my earliest experiences as an online trainer. I was a product trainer for Webex, so my topic was the technology and making it work for new clients. We always taught the classes alone, but the training team helped one another if we had a problem, and we had a direct instant messaging line to the IT team as well. It was important the clients had a positive experience with their new product and so we had systems in place to make a good impression and to make things work properly. Since my topic was the technology, I did not have an additional person in the session with me in the role of producer, but I did have people around me helping to produce a successful session. However, all of that changed when I went on to my next online training job: teaching trainers to be virtual trainers.

When the topic changed, the focus was no longer completely on the technology, and participants did not want me to spend time troubleshooting or explaining all that was happening if we were supposed to be learning presentation and facilitation strategies. They were happy to focus on it during the technology segments, but it became a waste of time if we had moved on to the other learning topics. I needed a producer to manage the technical side of things when I was not teaching about the technology, so the role became official among the training team and we began delivering sessions in partnership. Because these producers were also trainers, we developed processes where they not only managed the technology, but could also teach portions of the class if something was going wrong on my end, or if we simply wanted to add a different perspective and voice to the content of the program. The facilitative virtual classroom training producer was born.

Some virtual training sessions may only involve a technical producer because a facilitative producer was not available, or the session does not need or benefit from having two trainers. Be aware that when teaching a live online training session with a facilitative producer, it will likely be more of an investment of your time given the elevated responsibility of their role, so it is important to plan. Here is generally what to expect when working with a facilitative producer for your virtual classroom training:

- An email confirming the topic, date, time, and link to the session as well as a written introduction to the person producing if you have not previously met them.
- A request for an introductory call to meet and learn about one another and to review the topic and instructional approach of the training.
- A request for all training materials including a trainer's manual, notes, presentation materials, and participant materials so the producer can review and learn them. A recording of any previous deliveries of this content may also be requested.
  - The training materials should include a clear outline of what is expected of the producer and how each feature will be managed: script, introductions, timing, chat, polls, breakouts, whiteboards, breaks, and so on.
- A request to share contact information and backup plans for alternative connections should something go wrong on the day of the session.
- A date, time, and link for a technical rehearsal. Fifteen to 30 minutes is the average time, and all systems, connections, hardware, and software will be tested.
- A date, time, and link for an instructional rehearsal, which may or may not be at the same time as the technical rehearsal. The average time is at least half the time of the scheduled training, but can be the same amount of time as the entire duration of the training.
- A reminder to join from the same computer, location, connection, hardware, and software that was used on the day of the technical rehearsal.
- A request to join the training at least 15–30 minutes in advance of the start time on the day of the session, including a final sound and system check.
- An announcement that there will be a recording if one is being made.
- A formal ending announcing that the recording has ended and the session is complete.
- Roster tracking and updating is also often handled by the producer.

Start-Time Producers

These are people who assist online meetings, webinars, and virtual training sessions only in the beginning to help everyone connect and get the session off to a good start. They do not stay for the entire session but do often remain available to be called back in if assistance is needed.

While I hope by this point it's clear the value a separate producer adds, the extra person is often still viewed as a luxury rather than a necessity. This book has attempted to outline all the production tasks you need to consider in order to be successful, but you may still find yourself in a situation where you cannot hire a person to produce your sessions, and that brings us to the final, session-saving type of producer: the start-time producer.

Most technical problems happen at the time participants are trying to first connect to the session. The two most difficult technical issues are accessing the web conferencing software or session itself and connecting to the audio. The first moments of any online session are not only the most fraught with technical problems, but also the most important time to make a positive first impression on the attendees. Given these two reasons, appointing someone in the role of a start-time producer will be highly beneficial for everyone involved.

When working with a start-time producer, be sure to share all session details with them including the topic, date, time, duration, link, and audio information. Designate them in the role of alternate or co-host so they have access to troubleshoot and assist with everything necessary to provide proper technical assistance to anyone who needs it. If your session only permits one host-type role at a time, then open your session at least 30 minutes to an hour early, grant them the role of the host, and then once the start-time producer is no longer needed, have them pass the role back to you to run the rest of the session.

I have found it most effective to have the start-time producer in a live session with me for the 15–30 minutes before a session, and at least 15 minutes after it begins. They should obviously stay in the session for as long as technical support is needed, but those first 15 minutes are the most crucial.

And finally, remember start-time producers could be anyone on your team or in the organization who has the knowledge and skills to help participants get connected to a live online session.

* * *

Whether a webinar, virtual classroom training, or online meeting, the three producer types are all technically skilled first. Because facilitative producing requires additional presentation and training skills as well as preparation time to learn the content and topic, they are the only type that could swap roles with the presenter or trainer in the session of a problem where a backup presenter was needed. Technical producers and designated start-time producers are not ever expected to do that, and a session that had a problem with a presenter would simply need to wait for the problem to be resolved or for the session to be rescheduled.

No matter the type of producer, a walk-through, a dry run, or what is most often called a "rehearsal" is required. Let's examine this concept and the details around it.

Rehearsals

I've mentioned the concept—and usefulness—of rehearsals throughout this book. Webinars often call this a dry run. Meetings often refer to it as a walk-through. Virtual training sessions typically label them rehearsals, especially when working with an instructional producer. Whatever you call it, a rehearsal is always done in the web conferencing platform that will be used for the live session so that everything can be tested, taught, and confirmed.

There are three primary goals for a rehearsal: to perform technical checks, review the plan for the content, and build a successful working relationship between the producer and the presenter or trainer. For two people to work together in front of a live audience while managing technology, it goes without saying they need a strong working relationship. It is widely accepted that trust, teamwork, communication, and respect are keys to this being successful, so focusing on this in a virtual environment begins from the first email and carries through during each subsequent meeting, with the rehearsal arguably being the most important.

Perform Technical Checks

As referenced in the earlier lists on what to expect when working with another person in the role of the producer, the technical check is the first and foremost task of any rehearsal. The internet connection, the computer, and the audio connection need to be tested well in advance of the live session date. The "well in advance" is important because technical support might be needed beyond a setting change, possibly requiring escalated assistance or administrative access. Additionally, people may need to obtain new equipment, such as when a microphone, headset, or webcam is not working properly. It's also important that presenters share any materials and applications during technical rehearsal to confirm everything is working and can be seen clearly.

Once the basic technical checks have been tested and confirmed to be in working order, it is also important to test the features being used for all the activities that are planned. This leads to the next part of the rehearsal, the content of the presentation or training.

Review the Plan for the Content

Presenters and producers should agree on who is doing what and at what time. If a presenter is delivering a webinar, they should send the producer a copy of the slides, any polls needed, and any handouts or files for the participants. During the rehearsal, the presenter and producer should walk through the presenter notes, determining the timing and even practicing saying the transitions out loud. The producer should explain the opening sequences and practice the verbal handoff to the presenter so they are clear on when they should begin speaking and moving their slides.

This gets to a pet peeve of mine that so many presenters commit: No one is engaged hearing you repeat "next slide" for the 25 to 50 slides you likely have in your deck. Move your own slides! (Or rehearse with the producer so that you both know when to move forward without having to say that each time.)

Whether presenting a webinar or delivering a live online training, the delivery plan should have a placeholder for polls that clearly states when it is time for them so the producer knows exactly when to launch the poll, reveal results, and close them. I find it helpful to talk as if we are on a radio show, providing clear cues to my producer on what is going on and what should be happening at each moment. For example:

> [Presenter] Kassy: So for our webinar today, as we can see, there is much confusion over what we call training when it is delivered live online. In just a moment, [Producer] Dmitriy is going to open a poll we've prepared that lists a number of terms we have seen used over the years.

[Producer] Dmitriy: Thanks, Kassy, the poll is now open. Everyone, please take a moment to review the choices and we'll share the results shortly. [Waits until the results are in and then shares them.] The results are in, Kassy!

[Presenter] Kassy: "Thanks Dmitriy! I see we're in alignment here . . . most of us are calling it virtual classroom training, but look, virtual instructor-led training is only a few votes behind. Let's examine this further as we look into my formal definitions next.

In reviewing the plan for the content of a webinar, the producer and presenter should work through each segment, clarifying these types of verbal exchanges as well as how questions should be handled. It is an effective strategy to have the producer use the "raise hand" feedback tool when they want to interrupt a presenter while they are speaking. Presenters need to learn to pay attention to such indicators if they are working to be more effective at online presenting, and should also pause at planned times to inquire with the producer about the status of questions or comments they may have missed or that have come in that they did not or cannot see.

A content rehearsal for a live online training session is similar but likely more detailed as learning activities typically involve more instructions for participants, especially when breakout sessions are planned. The trainer and producer should have a copy of the trainer manual available so they can walk through each segment, testing that the features are working as planned for each learning activity. For example, testing webcams, running polls, testing chat and annotation tools, confirming feedback tools are in view, and even running through the sequence of the breakout room activities from start to finish. Participants are usually more involved in a training than they are a presentation so it is important for the person producing to know exactly when extra technical guidance may be needed.

Facilitative production rehearsals may be more detailed if the person producing has their own script or verbal instructions to provide throughout the session. Breakout activities tend to require verbal instruction on the activity from the trainer and technical directions from the producer on how to get to the breakout room to complete the assignment. (See chapter 7 for an example producer script to get participants into a breakout room activity.) Remember that it is important to work out who is doing what, for how long, and exactly at what time during these rehearsals. This will ensure the most effective and successful delivery of your live online session.

Practice the Producer's Speaking Voice During Rehearsal

Public speaking, appearing on camera, and controlling the tone of one's voice are all aspects of being a presenter. Not everyone with the technical support skills needed for the role of a producer also have the background, natural ability, or skill to be presenters. During rehearsal it is important to allow the person producing time to practice the public speaking part of their role. Following are some example introductory scripts, typical of the type of presenting a person producing will need to do. If you are a person producing, rewrite these to be applicable to your sessions, and practice saying them out loud while on camera during the rehearsal.

For a webinar: This is typically done as the webinar officially opens and it is time to begin. This introduction usually takes only a few minutes. It is worth noting that this same producer likely has had early attendees on a music hold and has come in periodically before the scheduled start time to make similar announcements thanking them and signaling how much time is remaining until start time.

"Hello and welcome to Five Keys for Successful Virtual Classroom Training with Kassy LaBorie. My name is John Sullivan, *[role and company]* and I am the producer for our webinar today. Our webinar is being recorded and the recording, along with the handout from today's presentation, will be made available in a follow-up email communication. We have enabled the Q&A for you today, as well as the chat *[add any other quick feature references here as well]*. We appreciate your time and interest in our presentation and want to take a moment to thank our sponsors *[names here]* and of course our presenter, Kassy LaBorie. *[Add the presenter's bio here.]* And now without further ado, Kassy LaBorie!"

For a training: This is usually done right after the trainer has done their introduction, is recommended to be done on webcam, and should only take about two minutes.

> "Hello, my name is Tabatha Michaels, and I'll be supporting today's session in the role of producer. This means I am here to support our trainer and you with the successful use of our live online training platform. Please use chat to message me with any technical concerns you may have, and follow along with me for the next few minutes as I show you around the basic features so you can participate in today's activities."

From there, the producer can proceed to teaching something like The Learning Launch as detailed in chapter 8 or verbally give the session back to the trainer to take the lead in the next segment of the class.

Rehearse the "Yes, and" Technique to Manage Changes to Plans

A producer's speaking voice is obviously important when communicating technical instructions and support, and is not usually rehearsed. But I have found it helpful to practice how changes to plans will verbally be managed during a rehearsal so there will be less confusion should it occur. Such changes can verbally be managed with the "Yes, and" technique.

"Yes, and" is an improvisational acting technique that suggests a conversational partner should accept what has been stated and then build upon it to continue the dialogue. Use the "yes, and" technique to manage conversations, transitions, or changes of plans with between presenters, trainers, and producers. This strategy is also quite helpful in moments where clarification is needed, or a change of plans must be communicated while managing a session in front of a live audience.

Let's say that you are producing a session for a presenter named Jack, and following a poll, he does not see that there are more responses that have been added to the chat. You might say something like this: "Jack, that is an interesting point you just made following the poll results. In the chat, our attendees have added additional insight. *[Verbally repeat a few.]* What is your response to those?"

Or maybe the breakout sessions won't launch, and the trainer, Evelyn, is waiting for the person producing to send everyone into them. This might sound like: "It turns out there needs to be a change in plans, Evelyn. The breakout sessions are not launching currently, so we are going to do this as a private chat activity instead. I've listed the partners in chat, so let's begin the activity by locating our partners and sending a private chat to them."

It's a leading practice to talk through these types of scenarios, rehearsing out loud the plan for each activity involving participants so presenters, trainers, and producers can get used to each other's way of speaking. It is also worth talking through a few alternative back-up plans using the "yes, and" technique.

Building Successful Virtual Working Relationships

The rehearsal process serves to help you practice technical knowledge and skills, and to establish a certain level of trust and confidence between presenters, trainers, and producers delivering sessions together. Smoothly managing through problems encountered, communicating changes in the moment, and giving one another feedback are important ways in which people working together can make the live online session effective, engaging, and memorable for everyone involved. It takes time to build such a relationship and it is best done through open lines of communication, detailed action plans, and live online experiences together. The more trust that is built between the two people, the better the session will be. A rehearsal is the perfect time to develop that trust.

Two of the most impactful relationships for me during my 20-plus year career as a virtual trainer and presenter have been with Elizabeth Rigney and Dmitriy Zolotykh. Elizabeth and I have delivered hundreds of training sessions together and have developed a level of trust where I would follow her lead without hesitation. After so many experiences together, positive and challenging, we've learned how we each prefer to work, what we each need to say to be best understood, and how to give one another feedback in a way that is helpful and effective. It has not always been easy, but by committing to communicating with one another and respecting each other's opinions, we created not only a working relationship, but also a lasting friendship. One of my favorite things to do while teaching online with her in the role of facilitative producer is to make her laugh when it is her turn to take the lead presenting. I do this by sending funny jokes to her in the private instant message group we have set up to run behind the scenes. She struggles to contain her laughter when I find a particularly good joke, and it has been a running thing between the two of us for years. I must be careful though, because she really is better at finding good jokes than I am so as soon as it's my turn, I have to watch out!

My working relationship with Dmitriy, who began as technical producer but then became a facilitative one, developed in much the same way as it did with Elizabeth: delivering hundreds of live online sessions together, sharing challenging and positive moments, and creating as many fun moments as we could. Dmitriy is particularly good at observing behavior and thoughtfully giving feedback, and through the years he has developed a way to share ideas and suggestions on ways I could improve or alter my delivery style for different situations. He can even do this—using the private instant messaging tool—while I am live with an audience. On more than one occasion, Dmitriy has coached me in the moment on things like timing ("You have one minute remaining") or delivering a clearer message ("Restate the question, asking them why they think it was challenging. They didn't get it the first time you asked.")

It is incredible to have this kind of support and camaraderie while presenting. It comes with years of dedication to building the relationship, trust, respect, and even some technical agility to manage a private message while delivering online.

A Team of Producers

Another important working relationship is the one between those who are in the role of producer or who have taken the lead on the production tasks. I have found this to be the most effective way for people to learn how to do the producer job quickly and efficiently, while having a little bit of fun at the same time. In all the virtual teams that I have either worked on or led, a primary way of communicating has been through an ongoing instant messaging program or chat channel, as mentioned in my previous examples with Elizabeth and Dmitriy. This was also referred to in chapter 5 as an effective way to manage technical support issues if a producer is stuck and needs help while live in session. Fostering working relationships between others who are performing production tasks is the most effective way for people to learn the ins and outs of live production. Who better to provide it than other producers while live in session, working through various troubleshooting actions together? All the training and preparation in the world does not compare to the real thing happening in real time with others helping you through it. This relationship is powerful.

Microsoft Teams and Slack are examples of this type of online communication tool. In your collaboration or messaging tool, you can create a channel just for producers so they can have a space to ask technical questions of one another and to share what they learn about the different platforms as they experience supporting them. These chat channels serve as a particularly effective way for producers to quickly call upon one another for additional support while live online. It is not realistic for a producer to have to hang up from a live session so they can call technical support. A chat channel is best, because it builds the skills of all the team members at the same time. They end up troubleshooting together and calling upon one another to do research or simply lend a helping hand. Figures 9-1 and 9-2 show two example exchanges demonstrating how quickly support occurs as well as how fondly the exchanges between team members can be, which is especially important during times of high stress.

Figure 9-1. Producer Chat Channel (Example #1)

Figure 9-2. Producer Chat Channel (Example #2)

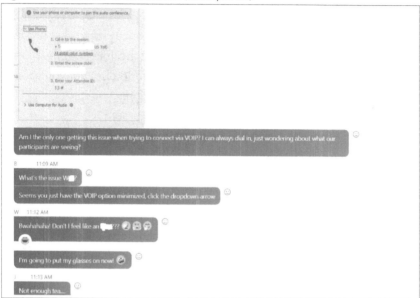

Conclusion

Making sure that facilitators and producers form strong partnerships is one of the most important decisions an organization can make toward the success of any virtual training or webinar strategy. All producers are technical, but not all will be able to help present or teach. It's important to manage expectations and make plans for the type of online session you are conducting, whether you are the presenter, trainer, or person producing. In the next chapter, we'll examine the administrative settings available in most web conferencing platforms. These back-end settings determine how all the hosts will use your site and how the many features come together to allow a team to build and create engaging live online experiences.

Reflection Questions

▸ Technical or facilitative: What is your preference and why?

▸ How will you convince presenters, trainers, and producers in your organization to conduct rehearsals?

▸ What relationship-building activities could you implement to help strengthen your working relationships?

Administration and Logistics

In This Chapter

- The web conferencing site, the settings, and the software
- Understanding your account and your login
- Stored content, reporting options, and mobile device downloads

It is unusual to have this happen in the same week, but I am not exaggerating when I say that on a Monday I was invited to a session where we were all attendees and on a Thursday I presented a webinar where all 250 of us were presenters. The "all attendees" session was a rehearsal with a client, and when the facilitator went to practice the breakout and there was no option, he realized he had joined the session as an attendee. He'd used the same link he sent for us to join, without signing into the administrative side of his account so he could host the session. He did not have access to lead the session, so he logged out and came back in as host, but even that did not fix the entire situation. He had not enabled the breakout feature from his site, so we still did not have breakouts. He had to enable the breakouts in his profile settings, end the session we were all in, create a new one, and get us all reconnected in the correct meeting, with the correct logins and settings.

And then on the Thursday of that week, I was invited to be a presenter at a webinar where all 250 people were sent the presenter link, just like me. All of them had control. They could all mute each other and they kept unmuting and muting throughout the hour, not realizing they were affecting everyone. They kept taking control from me and stopping my screen share. They even removed me from the session once. I had to reconnect and reshare five times, but I survived, presenting despite these problems. The people who scheduled this session and the all-attendee rehearsal learned a tough lesson about the administrative side of producing a live online session: Know your options, learn the details.

To wrap up this book, let's turn to the less heralded aspects of producing virtual instructor-led training, online meetings, and webinars: administration and logistics. Previous chapters introduced you to the capabilities you need to produce a smooth virtual session, the features you need to know and how to troubleshoot them, and then the preparation and design elements to consider when planning how the session will go. You're nearly ready to play your part turning passive attendees into active participants. But before you start your next live online session with an expectant audience, you should be aware of a few additional administrative, communications, and logistical features critical to production as well as the follow-up tracking and reporting tasks to complete the process of your sessions.

Whether your platform is a builder or revealer type, it is still necessary to have a designated session leader–level login to schedule and set up online sessions. The most common term used by the online meeting platforms is "host," so for the remainder of this chapter, that's what I'll use. Regardless of the name, this level of login must have the correct credentials to sign in, schedule, and lead live online meetings, trainings, and webinars. Builder platform types tend to have more space for storing and sharing content than revealer platform types, but they both have many options for the setup, preparation, and follow-up of your online sessions.

Getting Started

The ACT learning process (access, click, and team up) introduced in chapter 3 will be helpful when learning the administrative options available in your platform. At a high level there are seven steps to understand and follow to properly manage the administrative side of your account. The first step is understanding how your site is accessed, whether from the platform's website, through your learning management system, or via another way specifically designed and managed by your organization. Determining your specific login and ensuring it has the correct credentials comes next. Third is managing your profile, uploading a picture or logo if possible, and setting such details as passwords, an email address, a time zone, and perhaps a phone number.

Once the login is set up, it becomes important to locate where to schedule, edit, delete, and start your live online sessions. Given the importance of audio connections for online sessions, it is critical to understand how the audio is connected and expected to run once the session is live with an audience. The last two steps are regarding the audience: how they are invited and managed, and if the features and content intended for use during the live session should be prepared in advance or managed afterward (like recordings and attendance tracking).

Here is a breakdown of the seven steps:

1. Access the site and its settings.
2. Log in with the proper credentials.
3. Set up or manage your profile.
4. Locate where to schedule, edit, delete, and start your live online sessions.

5. Determine whether audio is included or integrated through a third-party provider, and if it is computer audio, teleconference, or both.

6. Determine where and how attendees' invitations and, if applicable, accounts are located.

7. Identify additional capabilities like content, polling and testing, virtual labs, recordings, and reporting.

The details and guidelines here have less to do with the content a speaker will be sharing once a meeting, webinar, or live online training is live with an audience, and more to do with all that goes on behind the scenes. This is not to minimize what happens in front of that audience, but rather to call attention to the importance of learning each of these details so that the live delivery goes as planned. It is often the case that all the focus is placed upon the presentation or the delivery of the session itself, thus missing important setup details that can make or break an online session. These administrative and logistical details are yet another important set of production tasks necessary for the successful execution of an engaging and effective live online session.

Table 10-1 offers a quick reference for learning the administrative settings and features of your platform for your practical understanding. Please consult the help files and formal documentation of your platform and learning management system for an official definition of each. Last, you can refer to chapter 4 on the virtual platform roles and in-session features for a detailed breakdown of the features used to interact and engage with an audience.

Table 10-1. Administrative Features Checklist

✓	FEATURE	DESCRIPTION
	Site	The website from which the live online meeting, training, or webinar conferencing platform is hosted.
	Settings	The options for the site that determine what features are available in the web conferencing platform and how it functions.
	Software: Download vs. Web Client	The application that powers the web conferencing platform and whether it is downloaded or used via web browser.
	Login and Profile	The credentials to manage and use the site to schedule, edit, start, delete, or attend sessions, and the unique settings for the login identifying the individual or team using the site.

Session Scheduling	The section of the site where users can schedule, invite, edit, start, join, and delete sessions.
Email Integration	An add-in or a plugin that allows easy scheduling of online sessions from your email program.
Audio	Connection to the broadcast, teleconference, or computer audio to hear and speak in a live online session.
Polling and Testing	A place to create and store survey and test questions to be attached to meetings or run separately from them.
Content	An area on the site where materials can be stored for sharing among users.
Reports	A section of the site that provides account owners and admins with various account, meeting, and webinar statistics to review how the organization is using the platform.
Mobile Application	An application available for download in your device's app store allowing mobile device access to your online sessions.

The Site, Settings, and Software

As stated in the introduction of this book, web conferencing software allows people to deliver and participate in meetings, training, and other types of presentations using an internet connection. Software is needed in some form to interact and share content with attendees. The site is where the software can be downloaded or accessed.

The first order of business is to locate the site from which the platform is running: Zoom.us, YourCompanyName.webex.com, or YourCompanyName .adobeconnect.com are examples of what the URL might look like. The site URL and the way it is accessed depends on your organization and how they have decided to use the services. Web conferencing service providers usually offer the software as a time-limited free trial, a limited-feature free version that is not time limited, and various options for paid services that include more features and benefits like company branding and system integrations.

Access your site using the proper URL to best understand the full set of features and options available to you when setting up and managing your live online sessions. Note that some sites may be accessed internally through your company's intranet, a designated portal, an integrated email program, or other internal systems. This is usually the case for not only ease of use with single sign-on functionality in an organization, but also to manage an organization's security protocols.

Most web conferencing software is downloaded to your computer via an internet connection. A full download of the software is typically required to have access to all features and functionality of the platform. This is normally the preferred option for those hosting and presenting sessions as they likely want full access to all the capabilities to create an engaging and effective delivery of their content.

However, attendees may not be permitted to download software on their computers without privileges or security controls that allow this to happen. Therefore, most of the web conferencing providers also offer a web client version of their platform. This version does not require attendees to download anything to participate in a live online session, but it also offers fewer features available for their use. If a feature is not working or seemingly missing from your options, check to see if you are using the web client version of the software. (Remember this too if a participant presents this problem to you.) It is likely the reason unless that feature has been disabled from your site's settings or in the specific session you are running.

A site administrator—or the person who has the primary control of the web conferencing account—has the highest level of access and will determine how the site operates and other settings that will be available for users to access when running online sessions. For example, a site administrator can not only approve user accounts, but also determine such settings as whether passwords are required or optional when scheduling sessions. They also have access to reports providing data on how the site is being used by all of its users. Determine who the site administrator is for your organization, so you know who to go to in case you have questions about how the site operates or requests for changes or additional privileges.

The site administrator can also explain exactly how the web conferencing software and platform are working within your specific environment. It is not uncommon for a company to choose to customize how the web conferencing platforms work within their environment, so do not be alarmed if the standard help files or articles posted on the internet do not apply to your site. Check with your site administrator for your specific set of circumstances, privileges, and overall settings.

The Login and Your Account Profile

Beyond the site administrator, other roles variously include hosts, organizers, presenter, panelists, and attendees to name a few (these roles were detailed further in chapter 4.)

A login and password are normally required to access the web conferencing site. This login, sometimes referred to as a user ID or an account, will determine the level of access and control available to use the platform, such as to schedule and set up live online sessions. Typically, a login is unique and connected to the individual's or team's email address.

Host-level access will allow a person to set up and schedule sessions, determine who and how to invite attendees, and manage content connected to it, recordings, reports, and other settings. Presenters may or may not need designated logins, depending on the platform, but they may be sent special presenter invitations with links that promote them to their presenter status upon joining the session.

A login may or may not be required of attendees. It depends on the platform you are using, but some like Adobe Connect allow hosts to designate an attendee account for people who are participating in sessions. This would allow users to see things such as a calendar of all sessions they are registered for or invited to and can immediately join each. Even if these sites do not require attendees to have accounts, make note of this option to see if it would be helpful for you to use. If your company uses a learning management system or other type of learning portal, this may not be necessary as that type of information is likely being managed from that system instead.

If you are given a login to your company's web conferencing site, look for a place to click on your profile and confirm the settings are correct and to your liking. It may be a link that simply says "Profile" or "My Profile," but regardless it will be a place for you to enter such details as your name, email address, password, phone number, time zone, and language preferences. Including your phone number in your profile will be useful if using an integrated teleconferencing program for the audio portion of your sessions. The number listed in the profile typically auto-populates when opening the session, saving you the time of having to manually enter it. This will also likely be where additional integrations with third-party services or applications such as email and calendar programs will be located. Most profiles also permit users to upload a picture that will display in the participants panel of the live session when that person is not using their webcam. Some users may choose to share a login at their organization, in which case these profile settings may be a team name and logo rather than a person's name and picture.

After receiving your login to a site and setting up your personal profile, be sure to click on any other setting options available. In Zoom, for example, nonverbal feedback, polling, and file transfer are just a few of the options that must be enabled on each user's profile settings. The features are there, but not all of them are turned on by default for all users. The site administrator often determines first what is available, and then each user may go in and change settings and options for themselves, so they have choices when running their own meetings, training sessions, and webinars.

Session Scheduling, Email Integration, and Audio Types

The host or organizer schedules and sets up new live online sessions. The details like a topic, date, time, duration, and audio information are all determined when scheduling the sessions. A login to the site is required in order to set up and schedule sessions, but that doesn't mean you can only do so using a web browser. A downloaded version of the application can often be used, and in some cases, sessions can be set up directly from an integrated email or calendar application. However, note that these desktop applications or email or calendar integrations may have fewer features available for setting up your sessions. For example, with Webex, the meeting product is generally integrated with the email program, rather than the training product. So, to schedule a session that will use Webex Training Center, you need to access the site directly instead of using your calendar.

At the time you are scheduling your live online sessions, you will usually see options for sending invitations to attendees and presenters. These invitations will include the link to join, the topic, date, time, duration, password, and sometimes links to test the systems in advance. If the email invitation does not include details like a test meeting or other information you would like, then consider sending yourself a copy of the invitation that you can customize and forward using your own email program and processes.

Requesting that attendees register for your session is also usually an option. Registration invitations will include information about the session and a link to register to let you know they intend to join. Webinars often use this feature as they usually invite large numbers of people to the session expecting that only a fraction of them will be able to attend.

Also included when scheduling sessions is the date, time, and optional recurrence of the sessions. Some platforms have detailed settings for creating sessions that will allow for reoccurring single sessions, multiple session seminars, and even irregularly occurring dates and times.

Some sites even allow for pre-session management of breakout room assignments, polls, tests, labs, and other shared content as well as session materials and handouts. Check with your specific site to see if these options are available, and then determine if they are necessary depending on what systems are in place for the scheduling and marketing of your live online sessions.

When scheduling sessions, determine the type of audio that will be used during the live session. (The details for how audio functions once a session is live are in chapter 4.) Your platform may have audio that is integrated, or it may not have that option at all. If it is integrated, at the time a host is setting up the session, they will likely have a field where they can decide if teleconference, computer audio, or both will be available to participants once they join the session. If audio is not integrated with the platform you are using, you will need to determine how participants will be hearing and speaking in the live online session you are hosting. A separate teleconference line may need to be set up and run at the time of the live session, and if it is not integrated, participants will not see any buttons or windows to click on to connect to the audio. However, this has become increasingly rare in the past few years as most web conferencing providers now have integrated options for audio.

The integrated options for these choices are first set by the site administrator, and then chosen by each host individually as they schedule the sessions. Some platforms and sites, like Adobe Connect, require host accounts to connect audio profiles in the audio section of their login. Third-party teleconference providers supply the dial-in numbers for the online sessions, and each host needs to add their specific teleconference credentials to their profile so the sessions they schedule will have the correct teleconference information attached to them. Again, check with your platform for specific details on setting up and connecting the teleconference and computer audio options for your live online sessions.

Polls, Tests, and Other Content Options

Creating polls, setting up tests, and accessing other prepared materials are other options often available on the web conferencing platform site. These features, if they are available, help make the preparation and planning of a live online session more efficient. Most platforms, at least those that support a polling or testing feature, have a location where you can create the questions and answers in advance and then connect them to the session. Some platforms even allow for sharing of such files, allowing multiple hosts of the site to use the same polls repeatedly as needed. This is an incredible time saver for an instructional design team, allowing them to create all the polls and tests and place them in a library of sorts, so they can be attached to sessions when they are run live with each new cohort or group of attendees. An example of one such poll would be a standardized feedback survey; an example of a test would be one connected to a compliance training that is run on a regular schedule for different groups of people. In such cases, hosts will not need to recreate the survey or the test each time. Webex Training Center has this feature, as does Adobe Connect, so check your account to see what options exist for your login.

Another option on a site, especially if it is a builder platform type, is an area for content like PowerPoint presentations and other files to be shared across users. This useful feature allows you to upload an entire course curriculum, and then connect to or pull it into live sessions as needed. Adobe Connect has an entire content section that many organizations use for this reason. It enables hosts to quickly access shared materials for meetings, training sessions, and webinars. Not all sites have this feature, so again, check to see what is included with yours.

Reports for Tracking Usage and Other Data

Another important feature available in most web conferencing software platforms is reporting. Site administrators typically need access to usage reports for a variety of reasons, ranging from data on the number of meetings being conducted, attendance to sessions, recording access and space usage, and the numbers of hosts using their accounts. Most platforms enable site administrators to collect data across the entire site for all users, and for individual hosts to access reports on usage from their own accounts.

The most common repots used by hosts are on attendance, allowing them to see who attended and often for how long they remained in the session. Webinar hosts use registration reports to collect user information and know exactly who is attending the webinar. The attendance reports can be compared against registration reports to analyze data on how many sign up versus how many attend. Recording reports help hosts understand whether there is value in providing recorded access to sessions. Some systems have reports on polling and testing data, allowing hosts to analyze and share that data as it pertains to the organization's needs and session details.

Access to such reporting data allows a better understanding of the investment made in the web conferencing service.

Mobile Application Versions

Attending an online meeting or webinar from a mobile device is not only convenient but also an increasingly common way to participate. Almost every web conferencing software provider today has a mobile version available for attendees who want to access their sessions from a phone, tablet, or other mobile device. The mobile versions of the software are usually available from the application store connected to the specific mobile device in use. Attendees must download the mobile application before they can participate in their live online session.

The mobile applications are similar to the web client versions of the software in that they often do not have the full set of features and functionality available, but do permit attendees to have a successful experience seeing and hearing the information being shared in the session. As a result, the mobile version of the web conferencing software (at the time of this writing) is typically not advanced enough for session leaders, but things continue to change each day in our world of technology, so keep an eye out for new advancements.

Conclusion

Expert Production Masters, that is what you have become. Having focused on what it takes to learn the web conferencing and live online training and meeting platforms, you are ready to take on the exciting adventure of producing engaging live online sessions. There are, as you now know, two main types of platforms—Builders and Revealers—and many feature options within each of them. When working on your own meetings, webinars, and training sessions, or helping others make the most of theirs, your skills will not only be sought out but coveted by many!

Besides knowing what the technology can do, you also know how to best support it should things go wrong, like a poll not launching, or creating alternative solutions if the breakouts are not working. Beyond knowing the details of how to provide support during these sessions, you also know the importance of the design and planning of sessions so producers, presenters, trainers, meeting leaders, and participants are all set up for success.

All the technical knowledge and skill is only as good as your ability to communicate it to others and your attention to those people skills will be what separates you from others who have been called upon to support a session. Further, developing partnerships and great working relationships with others who are delivering and supporting live online sessions will sharpen your skills and strengthen your network. I wish you great success with your virtual training, meeting, and webinar production. See you online!

Reflection Questions

▸ What is the URL for your site and what is your login?

▸ What are the audio choices for your account?

▸ What options does your platform offer for mobile device access? How do you download these and what differences do you notice with the interface?

Acknowledgments

Production in this book's context is the art of support—the support of technology and the people using it to bring everything planned together in a way that makes all of it appear effortless. This book is about the supporting tasks and role of a person who spends their time making sure everyone has what they need, and everything is in its place—the person who spends their time thinking of the needs of others. It is with this in mind I want to formally acknowledge all those who have produced webinars and virtual training sessions for me as well as those who have extended their patience, encouragement, and love to help me to produce this book!

There have been countless producers in my two decades of presenting and training online who inspired the stories, processes, examples, and ideas in this book. I thank each and every one of you for your technical expertise, patience, and creativity. Some of these delightful people include Dmitriy Zolotykh, Joe Murray, Brendan Shields, Sonia Furini, Mike Morneau, Luke Chiaruttini, Julie Miller, Helen Fong, Staci Tousignant, Clare Davis, Jerry Chiea, Kara Roche, Jacqueline Ferras, and Elizabeth Rigney to name just a few. You know I'll be reaching out to you as long as we get to deliver these live online events and the internet keeps us connected!

So many learning and development colleagues, mentors, and friends have encouraged me to write and share my experiences, and I want to extend a heartfelt thank you to the following people for listening, inspiring, and often brainstorming: Cynthia Clay, Cindy Huggett, Nanette Miner, Elaine Biech, Jo Cook, Brent Schlenker, Halelly Azulay, Betty Dannewitz, Leslie Rawlins, Therese Owen, Jo Cook, Joann Lynch, Kevin Thorn, and Wendy Terwelp.

ATD and the team of people who have edited and published this book are marvelous. I want to especially thank Justin Brusino for believing in me, and Jack Harlow for your insight, encouragement, guidance, and of course for putting up with me throughout this entire process!

I also want my friends and loving family to know that your support through this has been invaluable, even though I could not get together with everyone as often. Mom, George, and Ashley—you might not have known what my book was about until recently, but I know you care for me and wanted me to succeed no matter what I was writing about for hours on end!

My son, Wyatt, your ideas on how to organize some of the technical topics, and our bets on who could get our writing done first kept me going many a late night. You graduated high school with honors writing your essays, and I get to remember writing alongside you every time I look at my book. Luna and Speedy, my cats, thanks for keeping my feet warm and the air full of your purring sounds as I typed away.

And finally, I thank you with everything that I am, Tom Stone. You listened, edited, inquired, supported, guided, pushed, and cared for me in all the perfect ways throughout the entire process of completing this book. You are my partner in all things and the most splendid husband a gal could ever dream of.

Appendix

Here are a few example participant communications for live online training sessions. These are typically emailed to participants and sometimes also posted to an internal learning platform or other social media site used for the program. Anything italicized is meant to be customized for your programming and audience needs, but you should of course make additional edits to align with your program as needed.

Example Welcome Email

It is a good idea to send an email of this type at least one week in advance of a training session.

Purpose: To welcome participants to a program and provide important introductory details to set them up for success.

Details to include:
- A greeting and reiteration of the topic
- Introduction of the presenter, trainer, producer, or speaker
- A brief description of the program
- The program objectives
- Dates and times of the session or sessions
- Recommendations on how to set up the environment for the best possible experience
- Materials for the program that also might include handouts, participant manuals, pre-reading, or any required pre-work and assignments
  - This might include instructions for logging into a learning management system or similar site where assignments and other content are available

- The link to join the live online session
- Technical details including system requirements, internet connections, and audio details (for example, if a headset is needed or if it will be a teleconference)
- Contact information if support is needed

Note: If I am conducting a virtual training session, I do not include the teleconference information in the welcome email or the link to join via a mobile application. I inform participants that they need to join from their own computer, their own desk, and their own audio connections to fully participate. I do not want them to join via the phone and then just listen in to the training. However, if it is a webinar or a meeting where it would be OK to simply listen in, then I do include that information. The point is to communicate how participants should join so they know, and you can create the intended experiences.

Here's a template you can use:

Subject: Welcome to the Online Virtual Facilitator Certificate!

Greetings everyone!

It is such a pleasure to be meeting you in email and in our *[session next week]*. My name is *[trainer/presenter/producer]* and together with *[trainer/presenter/producer]* we will be the team partnering with you to help you create and launch your *[live online training]*. Get ready to work, to learn, to grow, and to have fun doing it!

PRE-READING: The Hard Truth, You Aren't Engaging.

I've attached an article I wrote for the February 2019 edition of ATD's *TD* magazine. Please read the first three pages and come to session 1 ready to share your thoughts on the ideas and processes offered.

TECHNICAL DETAILS AND PARTICIPANT MANUAL

Important: Make sure to join the session from your own computer and desk. A headset while using your phone or computer audio is most effective if you have one. I use this one from Logitech for my computer audio: amzn.to/2W2n1DS. We'll also be on webcam, so be ready to wave hello to one another. Most of our sessions are two hours, with a break in the middle. Bring water, coffee, tea, snacks, or whatever you need!

Also attached is your participant manual. In it you will find more information about the program, a place to follow along and take notes each time we meet, and your application assignments throughout the program. Plan for one to two hours of independent time to work on your application assignments following each session.

Also, please ensure you have done the following before the first session:

- TEST your computer and connection to Zoom: zoom.us/test
- Print the attached Participant Manual
- Join the session at least 10 minutes before start time so we can start (and end!) on time

DATES AND TIMES
Most sessions are two hours in duration unless otherwise indicated and are listed in EASTERN US time.

- S1: 3/16, 9–11 a.m.
- S2: 3/19, 9–11 a.m.
- S3: 3/23, 9–11 a.m.
- S4: 3/30, 9–11 a.m.
- S5: 4/3, 8–10 a.m.

LINK TO JOIN ALL THE SESSIONS: [add link here]

IMPORTANT: Please plug in your computer audio headset prior to joining the session. You may join using computer audio or telephone.

TIP FOR SUCCESS

Create a folder for emails from me. The follow-up communications for each live session will always have extra reading and resources. I'll also recap your assignments and give you the link to the recording of our sessions. All communications and files will be referred to in my emails for easy and quick reference.

Reach out with your questions, comments, and concerns. We look forward to our program!

Sincerely, Kassy

Example Reminder Email

One day in advance, and perhaps one hour before the session begins, send the same information that is in the welcome communications, but shorten it to include only the immediate needs, like the login, link, how to join, and the participant materials.

Purpose: To remind participants about their upcoming session.

Details to include:

- A reminder and reiteration of the topic, date, and time
- The link and the password, if necessary
- The technical details and requirements
- The environment and any other expectations

Here's a template you can use:

Subject: Reminder: Online Virtual Facilitator Certificate!

WE ARE LOOKING FORWARD TO MEETING EVERYONE SOON!

[Trainer/Presenter/Producer] and *[Trainer/Presenter/Producer]* wanted to provide you with a reminder of our live online session, *[date and time]*.

TECHNICAL DETAILS AND PARTICIPANT MANUAL

Important: Make sure to join the session from your own computer and desk. A headset while using your phone or computer audio is most effective if you have one. I use this one from Logitech for my computer audio: amzn.to/2W2n1DS. We'll also be on webcam so be ready to wave hello to one another. Most of our sessions are two hours, with a break in the middle. Bring water, coffee, tea, snacks, or whatever you need!

Also attached is your participant manual. In it you will find more information about the program, a place to follow along and take notes each time we meet, and your application assignments throughout the program. Plan for one to two hours of independent time to work on your application assignments following each session.

Also, please ensure you have done the following before the first session:

- TEST your computer and connection to Zoom: https://zoom.us/test

- Print the attached participant manual
- Join the session at least 10 minutes before start time so we can start (and end!) on time

LINK TO JOIN: [add link here]

IMPORTANT: Please plug in your computer audio headset prior to joining the session. You may join using computer audio or telephone.

Reach out with your questions, comments, and concerns and we will see you online soon!

Sincerely, Kassy

Example Follow-Up Email for Multi-Session Training Programs

These types of emails are recommended for training sessions that are in a series and help to keep participants on track during multipart programming. They serve as a brief wrap-up of what occurred and a reminder for what is to come next.

Purpose: To follow up with and remind participants what just occurred and what they are supposed to do between sessions if it is a multi-session program.

Details to include:

- A brief review of the session they just attended
- The link to the recording
- The details on next steps including application assignments
- Any additional resources or readings applicable to their learning
- The link or how to access the next session

Here's a template you can use:

Subject: Follow-up to Session 1: Online Virtual Facilitator

Greetings everyone! It was wonderful to connect with each of you today in session 1 of the Online Virtual Facilitator Certificate. I look forward to learning more about your online training and sharing in your successes as you continue to grow your virtual training skills. Attached are the screens I saved from today and a handout for your application assignment.

Recording: *[add link here]*

Session 1 Application Assignment

List the instructions and any reference materials here.

Additional Reading: *Articles, Videos, and More*

List the details or links to the additional resources here.

Please reach out if you have questions. I am happy to assist as you learn more about the platform.

Thank you! Kassy

Example Final Completion of Training Email

The following email is an example of the messaging shared with participants who have completed a live online training program where multiple sessions were involved as well as assignments and a final project.

Purpose: To finalize a program and congratulate participants who have competed it. This email also alerts managers and other leaders or decision makers to the successes of those participating.

Details to include:
- A congratulatory message of what was earned
- A survey of the experience for feedback collection
- Final certificates
- A link or access to the recording
- Next steps and words of encouragement

Here's a template you can use:

Subject: CONGRATULATIONS! You've completed the Online Virtual Facilitator Certificate!

Congratulations! You have SUCCESSFULLY COMPLETED the Online Virtual Facilitator Certificate with Kassy LaBorie Consulting. You have worked hard to learn how to proudly facilitate engaging and effective live online training! I am going to miss meeting with you each week. Promise to stay in touch! Complete page 32 in your participant manual— your action plan! Note the ideas that stood out for you, make a point to commit to actions, and continue to practice with Zoom and any other live online training tool you end up using. It's only up from here!

I've attached your feedback from the practice activities that we added to the chat at the end of each presentation. WAY to GO on those! You may add your certificate of completion to your LinkedIn profile by following the instructions on the attached .pdf file. I can also create .pdf version of your certificate that you can print if you'd like. Just let me know via email.

Survey for Feedback

It's been a pleasure to get to know you and work together. Your feedback about the program will help me to improve it moving forward. This survey only has three questions and should take a few minutes to complete. Thank you! [Include the link here]

Recording: [add link here]

Thank you again and I can't wait to hear about your next live online training adventure! Connect with me on LinkedIn at linkedin.com/in/kassylaborie to stay in touch! I love hearing about your online successes. I will miss meeting with you—you are an incredible team! Thank you for allowing me to join you on your virtual training journey.

Sincerely, Kassy

Index

Page numbers followed by *f* and *t* refer to figures and tables respectively.

About the Author

Kassy LaBorie is the founder and principal consultant at Kassy LaBorie Consulting. She is a virtual classroom master trainer specializing in developing trainers to be engaging and effective when facilitating programs in platforms such as Zoom, Webex, and Adobe Connect. She has worked with many Fortune 500 firms in a wide range of industries and sectors, including hospitality, pharma, energy, government, NGOs, and nonprofits.

She also trains and coaches producers, the virtual classroom trainer's partner in effective facilitation, as well as instructional designers tasked with creating or converting content for virtual classroom delivery. And she advises learning and development leaders in areas like virtual classroom strategy, technology selection, and logistics. She has more than 20 years of experience in passionately helping organizations, learning teams, and training professionals successfully move to the virtual environment.

Since 2008, she has participated in over 100 industry conferences as a speaker, expert panelist, and workshop trainer. She is a regular presenter at such events as the ATD International Conference & EXPO, ATD Tech-Knowledge, *Training* Magazine's 125 Conference, TechLearn, Learning Solutions, and DevLearn. Prior to launching her consulting practice, she was the director of Virtual Training Services at Dale Carnegie Training, a consulting service that partnered with organizations to help them develop successful online training strategies. She was also the product design architect responsible for developing the company's live online training product and experience, which grew to be a $4 million dollar business in only a few years.

Prior to this, she was an independent master virtual trainer, a Microsoft software trainer, and a senior trainer at Webex, where she helped build and deliver training at the Webex University.

She co-authored *Interact and Engage! 50+ Activities for Virtual Training, Meetings, and Webinars* (ATD Press 2015).